THERE WAS A TIME

rock & roll in the 1960s in Charlotte and North Carolina

**Jacob Berger
&
Daniel Coston**

There Was A Time: rock & roll in the 1960s in Charlotte, and North Carolina

Written by Jacob Berger and Daniel Coston

Edited by Daniel Coston

Interviews by Daniel Coston and Jacob Berger

Front and back cover design by Greg Russell

Original Front and back cover design by Donny Fletcher

Layout by Greg Russell

Cover photograph of the Young Ages by Dave Long

Back cover photographs by Jim Schmid

Book copyright 2013, 2014 Jacob Berger and Daniel Coston

A Fort Canoga Press release, copyright Daniel Coston

The authors have strived to present the interviews to the best of their abilities,
and to present the facts as we understood them. Not everyone may view this information
the same way, and the authors and interviewees are not liable for those differences in opinion.

Table Of Contents

Introductions by Daniel Coston and Jacob Berger iv

CHAPTER ONE: The Sound Before the Storm 1

CHAPTER TWO: 1964, First Bands and First Gigs 14

CHAPTER THREE: 1965 and 1966 22

CHAPTER FOUR: A Song Called Abba 42

CHAPTER FIVE: Instruments and Gear 55

CHAPTER SIX: Memorable Shows 61

CHAPTER SEVEN: Western and Piedmont N.C. 68

CHAPTER EIGHT: 1967, a Changing Scene 81

CHAPTER NINE: Murder in My Heart for the Judge 97

CHAPTER TEN: On the Air 106

CHAPTER ELEVEN: Eastern N.C. Scene 115

CHAPTER TWELVE: 1968 into 1969 128

CHAPTER THIRTEEN: To the Seventies … and Beyond 144

CHAPTER FOURTEEN: We All Shine on 152

DISCOGRAPHY 156

INTRODUCTIONS

Daniel Coston

"When are you going to do a book on the scene I grew up in?" Jake Berger (as many of us know him) asked me that more than once, when I was working on a book about Charlotte's legendary Double Door Inn. The idea was daunting, but very tempting. I am a huge fan of the music of the 1960s, yet knew very little about the scene around here during that era. To my great enjoyment, I discovered that there had been quite a lot going on.

In the early stages of this book, I suggested that the book be more than just the music scene in Charlotte, and also cover what was going on throughout the state. Many Charlotte bands were touring the Carolinas by 1966, while bands in other towns in North Carolina were doing the same. All of these bands contributed to the growth of music in this state during that time, and it has been a pleasure to document their stories.

Much of this book still centers on the scene in Charlotte. While several cities in North Carolina are deserving of their own book on this subject, the stories of Jake Berger, his friends and fellow musicians in Charlotte are the emotional core of this book. The characters in this book will reveal their stories, as the book progresses. The goal of this book was to have these stories be more than just a travelogue of the various scenes during that time. These were real kids, experiencing the high and lows of growing up in the 1960s, be it in Charlotte, or elsewhere. Much like the music they were playing, life during that time took a lot of twists and turns, and I hope that this book reflects those times.

This book also focuses more on the Rock & Roll scene in North Carolina during the 1960s. Much of North Carolina's other musical genres, such as rhythm & blues, and beach music has been documented elsewhere. This book deals with that group of kids that discovered music as the British Invasion dawned. Rock & Roll that was learned, and played in spare rooms and their parents' garage, hence the term "Garage

Rock". Later, this music turned into psychedelia, and the beginnings of punk rock, but it all came from one remarkable era.

Sincere thanks goes out to Ken Friedman, whose three volumes of Tobacco A Go Go has helped to document the music that has recorded during that time. My thanks with research to Mike Dugo and his website, www.60sgaragebands.com, as well as Chris Bishop and www.garagehangover.com, www.southerngaragebands.com, www.45cat.com, Jack Garrett, Vance Pollock and Riffin on www.ashevillefm.org, the Carolinas Rock & Roll Rememberd Facebook page, as well as the writings of Richie Unterberger. I also want to acknowledge the excellent series done by Mike Britton about the Asheville scene for Mountain Xpress Magazine. The world needs more stories like that. Much of this music discussed here can be found at the aforementioned websites, on Youtube, and the Tobacco A Go Go series. Search it out, and find it. It's worth the trip.

Turn on, tune in, and turn it up.

Jacob Berger

About 15 years ago, I decided to act on a project that had until that time had only existed in my head. I put down an outline of what was to become this book, and there it sat for another 13 or 14 years! In the meantime, I had gotten to know Daniel Coston through various encounters that happened because I was playing with Phil Lee. Daniel and I found that we had much in common, in that we were both huge fans of the music that came floating out of neighborhood garages nationwide, inspired by the music of the "British Invasion", and then blended by rank amateurs, in a most rudimentary fashion, with American Rhythm & Blues.

Searching my memory, and that of many of the musicians of the day (who were then in their teens), we have delved into the past to try and uncover the vast and hugely vibrant music scene of Charlotte, and of the region. I knew that working with Daniel would be a pleasure because not only is he knowledgeable in this field, but also because, like me, he is a fan, not only a fan of the musical genre that was popular in the day but of the "whole shebang". The gear, the clothes, culture of the young, and most of all the music!

A few years ago, after continuously harassing him to write a book of garage bands, he and I decided to combine our energies and get this thing written, and into the public eye. I have to thank Daniel for "partnering up" with me for this book, without whom the outline might have sat indefinitely on the shelf. My thanks to Sally Nehrenberg for transcribing the endless tapes of the ensuing interviews, and all of the musicians for giving their time and pictures for this project.

When Daniel and I started planning this book, it was to be solely about the music scene in Charlotte, North Carolina during the 1960's. In particular, it was to be about the garage bands that lay in the realm of teenagers. I toyed with the idea of putting it in the form of a "historical novel", making up pretend people that were an conglomeration of different characters that we knew, or more precisely that I knew due to my age. We interviewed as many of the musicians as we could. Many of them were people that had spurred me on to play guitar, because I had been so impressed with them and their bands when I was in my early teens. Many have forged a name for themselves, and are well known both here in Charlotte, and abroad. In talking with the musicians, I found a great deal of common experience. I also found that certain things that I witnessed and was impressed with had either faded from their memories, or had not made enough impression on them to warrant a place in their memories.

All that aside, I have been dreaming of putting down these stories, the most formidable instances in my young and impressionable life at the time. I found that I couldn't do it in a novel type format, as more and more memories came back to me, and I found that I was only really able to get it all down if I wrote it down as I saw it. Many times, I am sure I had acquired, due to youth, various "misconceptions" of actual events, but even as twisted as they were via personal impression, they still bear the watermark of reality. What follows is not only the story of the teen music scene here during the 1960's, but also the story of how I saw life here in Charlotte during that time, with a backdrop of teenage garage bands flailing away incessantly in the background.

CHAPTER ONE
The Sound Before the Storm

JAKE BERGER: Times were so very different when I was growing up here. All the growing pains of the world were as prominent in Charlotte as in any major city of the world, albeit on a smaller scale and slower to fruition. On one side there was a whole group, the last group as it turns out, of baby boomers. Kids that had been given the things that their parents had mostly not had, because now the post-World War Two economy was picking up speed at an alarming rate. The technology had also advanced rapidly, and because of this there was time to spare. Now kids and young adults had time for "recreation"! Life was so much easier for this generation. They had loads of time to play, and more importantly, get more than the bare bones of an education. With all of this came more exposure to what was happening worldwide.

Jacob "Jake" Berger at 13.
collection of Jacob Berger

My family didn't get our first TV until I was in the second or third grade, around 1960, '61. There were two network channels that had the network programs on at night, along with network national news. The rest of the programming during the day, and some at night filled in by local shows. In the afternoons, we had Cartoon Carnival, hosted by Joey The Clown, and on Saturdays there was the Little Rascals Club, hosted by Fred Kirby. Fred had been instrumental along with the WBT Briarhoppers in the vibrant country & western scene that included bluegrass, string band and old-time music. Charlotte had been the country music capital for a good while before it shifted to Nashville.

DANIEL COSTON: *In the early 1950s, a number of musical genres began to emerge across the United States. On one end, artists such as Muddy Waters, Elmore James, B. B. King* and Howlin' Wolf were electrifying blues music. The blues genre had emerged in the early part of the 20th century, and evolved in the rural south and delta regions in the 1920s and 1930s. Electric blues began to build audiences in the late 1940s, led by the Chicago-based record label Chess Records.

On another end, there was another group of artists that shared some of the same blues influences, but added a swing to the rhythm that owed as much to the swing band era of the 1930s and '40s. For lack of a more original term, these two elements were brought together when it was coined Rhythm & Blues, or R&B, for short. Rhythm & Blues was popular throughout the south, and was beginning to spread to the national record charts.

One of these songs was "Rocket 88," recorded by Jackie Brentson, Ike Turner and the Rhythm Kings at Sun Studios in Memphis, TN in 1948. "Rocket 88" has since been credited as being one of the first Rock & Roll records, with its up-tempo beat, "play it loud" sound, and a distorted guitar sound, thanks to a damaged amplifier. The success of "Rocket 88," and blues artists such as Howlin' Wolf pushed Sun Studios owner Sam Phillips to start seeking out white artists that could help in that crossover. In a few short years, Elvis Presley, Carl Perkins, Roy Orbison, Jerry Lee Lewis, and Johnny Cash would emerge through Phillips' Sun Records label.

This merging of sounds was happening fast, and taking shape in many places. North Carolina-born Nappy Brown hit the national Rhythm & Blues charts in 1954 with "Don't Be Angry." Written by Brown, the song incorporates rhythm & blues with a big band-like swing, while Brown sings with a calypso-like cadence. A few years later, Brown would re-arrange a standard entitled "The Night Time Is The Right Time," which would later become a huge crossover hit for Ray Charles.

By the mid 1950s, musical ideas seemed to be exploding everywhere. Some were drawn to the emergence of modern jazz. Others heard the harmony elements of Rhythm & Blues, and the pop music of the day, and began to create their own music of street corners and on record as doo-wop music. The electrified blues continued to evolve, taking in touches of American folk music with it. In term, white audiences became more involved with this new music, and began to claim it as their own. Cleveland-based DJ Alan Freed had first coined "Rock & Roll", after hearing some of his black listeners use the phrase as slang for sex, or "wild times."

Soon, white kids began to dance to these new records, and pick up guitars. One of the first sub-genres of Rock & Roll to emerge was Rockabilly. A hybrid of Rock & Roll, country music, and the still-relatively new bluegrass genre, Rockabilly required a few chords, a lot of energy, and some Elvis Presley-like vocals on top. Small record labels began popping up across the country, hungry to make money off Rockabilly, and the new *sounds of America. In every state, one could find a singer or group hoping for that big break. In North Carolina, some did find that success.*

Nappy Brown had a string of hits throughout the 1950s. Charlotte-born Wilbert Harrison had a number one hit in 1959 with "Kansas City," a song that would later be covered by the Beatles. Longtime Charlotte resident Maurice Williams saw his song "Little Darlin'" rise to number two in 1957 as a hit for the Diamonds. Williams and his own group, the Zodiacs would then strike gold on their own when their song "Stay" hit number one in 1960. Other notable stars of the R&B field to emerge from North Carolina in the 1950s included Clyde McPhatter, Ben E. King, and the 5 Royales. Another native North Carolinian, Link Wray influenced an entire generation of guitar players when his instrumental hit "Raunchy" hit the charts in 1958.

Also emerging from Charlotte, Arthur Smith had a hit with his syndicated Carolina Calling TV series Arthur Smith Studios. Smith had already had a huge hit in 1948 with his proto-rock hit "Guitar Boogie," and would go on to hit the charts again in 1972 when his song "Dueling Banjos" was featured in the movie "Deliverance". In 1957, Smith opened the Arthur Smith Studios, a modern recording studio that would go on to be studio of choice for many artists. This included James Brown, who recorded his groundbreaking "Papa's Got A Brand New Bag" at Arthur Smith in 1965.

RUSSELL HODGE: Arthur Smith's show went up and down the East Coast. He was a household name.

DANIEL COSTON: *Record labels were also beginning to appear in North Carolina. Colonial Records had huge hits in the late 1950s with local artists like Andy Griffith and George Hamilton IV, and would continue operations until the mid 1960s. Also sharing recording space with Colonial on the UNC-Chapel Hill campus was Brooke Records, based in Asheville. The label found some regional success with the Bluenotes and their song, "I Don't Know What It Is." In Durham, Renown Records released many artists associated with Johnston County native Jim Thornton throughout the 1950s, and early '60s. Thornton hosted the popular Saturday Night Country Style TV show was a popular late-night staple. Renown's most successful releases were with Wayne Handy, whose three Rock & Roll singles for Renown picked up found some national distribution through other record labels.*

At the same time this was going on, a number of kids in Charlotte began to play music, drawn in by what they were hearing on the radio, on TV, or just in their own neighborhood. But all would eventually find their way towards a musical re-birth in the 1960s.

ZAN MCLEOD: Fred Kirby. He was my next-door neighbor. I lived next door to him for about ten years! From the time I was about six until the time I was about sixteen. And he had a Martin D-28 guitar! It was incredible! And that was the first guitar I ever played. He used to sit out in his backyard and tune it up and play, sit out there and play it, and I heard him out there one time and I said, "Wow, that is really nice." and he said, "You wanna play it, son?" And I said, "Yeah, sure!" And he'd show me a chord and let me play it for a minute.

And he took me to his TV show a bunch of times, and he took us up to Tweetsie Railroad. And we knew his daughter. She was about our age. Yeah, he was the first guitar player in Charlotte that I knew of, besides Arthur Smith, and he was my next-door neighbor!

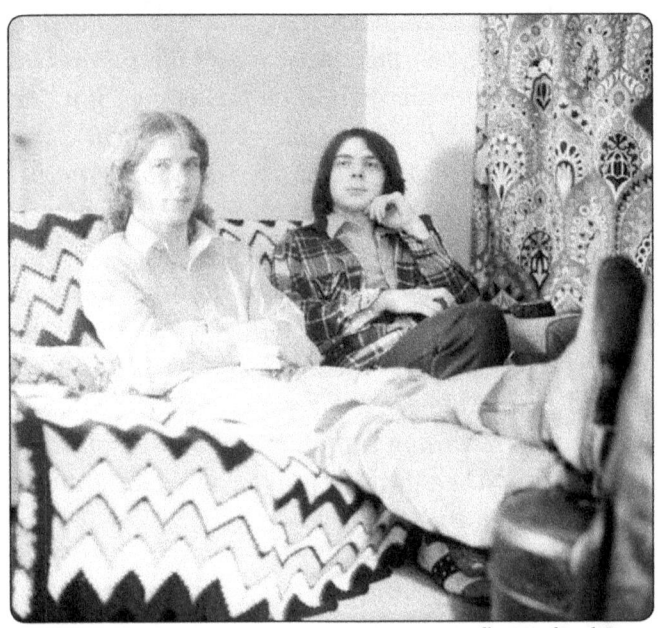

collection of Jacob Berger

Doug James (on left) with Ernie Ferreri, 1973.

DONNY FLETCHER: Cramerton was lucky enough to have a recreation swimming pool. You'd go down there, and someone would usually have a radio. You'd hear different songs, and then you'd have to out and find the record.

MARK MYERS: I started singing in chorus, in 7th or 8th grade. I had never sang before, and I enjoyed it. Plus, there were a couple of good-looking girls sitting next to me, and that didn't hurt.

GILL VANDERLIP: I wanted to play guitar when I saw James Burton play with Ricky Nelson! Everyone was looking at Ricky and saying how cute he was, but I wanted to know, "Who is that curly haired guy in the back playing all that cool guitar?" And Arthur Smith was in this town. He was a big influence, I used to watch him when I was six or seven years old, and he was a big influence in this town. He used to play Strat's and he also had a beautiful 335.

DAVID FLOYD: I was always interested in music, but my parents were not real interested in my doing that. I played trumpet in the marching band and the concert band. It was all brass. That's when I first got into music. That was when I was in the fifth grade.

DOUG JAMES: I was strumming badminton rackets when I was four. No one figured out that maybe I was destined to do this, you know? I began playing clarinet in fourth or fifth grade, whenever they let you start Band, and that was my first musical experience.

BOBBY DONALDSON: I was playing drums in a school band, and of course, my dad couldn't put up with that. So at Christmas all of a sudden, instead of a set of drums, here was a Silvertone guitar with the amplifier built into the case. And he could see that I was a little bit disappointed, so he said, "I know you wanted a set of drums, but I've heard you play drums and I just can't stand it. Here's a guitar, and if you are any good, you won't need lessons." Because he'd heard me play a few chords, just from picking it up from my aunt. So before I'd go to school in the mornings, picked up the needle and set it on a 45, and just learned it until I learned it.

ROB THORNE: The first time I played drums professionally was when I was twelve years old. That was 1955. I played New Year's Eve at the Elks Club, in downtown Charlotte with a dance band that were guys my dad's age. My dad was not on the bandstand that night, he was playing someplace else, and I don't remember who the band was. I had been going to Music Incorporated for a couple of years on Thursday nights. And from time to time they had jam sessions down there. All the big band guys that were retired. Music Incorporated was at the corner of Elizabeth Avenue and Independence Boulevard.

Douglas Furs was in the front. Ben Douglas owned that, and Bob Douglas, who was a drummer, owned Music Incorporated, which was in the back of that building. And I went down there for a couple of years with my dad whenever he would go, and I'd sit behind the drummer all night and watch the drummer play.

On my 12th birthday, in December, I got a drum kit for Christmas that my dad bought me, and we played on New Years Eve, and I've been playing ever since. I'm sure I was scared to death, playing with these old guys. They were my dad's age, and that time I bet he was in his forties, I believe. And he had played with Les Brown's Big Band during the day, and most of these guys had done it, in the 1930s, and this was in the Fifties.

There wasn't any Rock and Roll. These guys didn't play Rock & Roll at that time. It was all "legitimate" music. That's what they called it, "Strictly Legit"! My dad used to say it all the time, "I don't play any Rock & Roll."

BARRY STACKS: I grew up on this little on the Northeast coast of Massachusetts. It was called Cape Ann. When I was 13, there was a group of fellows that had been playing together for a while. They were a little older than me, and they needed a bass player. I had been playing guitar since I was eight or nine, so I went out and bought a bass and an amp, and taught myself to play. That was my first band, who were called the Galaxies. This was around 1958. We played venues around Boston, and north of Boston.

My grandparents, who raised me, died in the fall of 1958. My father invited me to move down to Charlotte to live with him. That was an eye-opener. You grow up on a New England island, and then you go to a cosmopolitan place like Charlotte. I got introduced to the music scene down there, and found it odd, compared to what I'd been used to. I pretty keep to myself, and played with just a couple of other guys, where we set up our amplifiers in one of our houses. I didn't play with another band again until the Grifs.

ROB THORNE: I think the first band I played with like that was a band called The Deltas. Some of those guys were in their twenties already. I was fifteen, and they would come and pick me up when we'd go to play gigs. And they were little gigs in Bessemer City, Gastonia, Mt. Holly. Right around the Charlotte area. Dance Clubs, they were redneck clubs, real hard-core kind of joints back then.

Whatever was popular at the time. Bo Diddley kind of stuff. But it was Pop. It was rock and roll for kids. Whatever they liked. And then I played with a band called the Jaguars after that. Because those guys knew a band from Forest City called the Jaguars. And I went to Virginia Beach that summer with them. I was sixteen. And I played all summer at Virginia Beach with the Jaguars. We played seven nights a week and matinees on Saturday and Sunday.

I had a duplex I lived in, expenses were paid and I think I made a hundred bucks a week. And my meals were covered for the most part and I thought, "I've died and gone to Heaven!" And my mom let me go! And these guys were older than I, and a worse influence than the other guys. And then that summer when I came back, a friend of mine who was in The Catalinas, their drummer was getting ready to go to college in September, and they asked me to come and audition and I joined the Catalinas that summer. That must have been '61.

The Catalinas, that was the first professional band I played with. I mean, I played with other professional bands, but that was the first "famous" band that I played with. And for a young kid, fifteen or sixteen years old, man, I thought that was great! Because we played all the time and I was making "real money" playing with these guys, and playing music that I loved and rubbing elbows with all these stars, and backing up all these major recording artists and groups that didn't travel with rhythm sections, they would hire the Catalinas to back them up, because we knew all the material. It was just a great time.

DANIEL COSTON: *Elvis Presley played the Carolina Theater in the early part of 1956, as the opening act on the country music package tour. He would return in the late summer of 1956 as the headliner at the newly opened Charlotte Coliseum, a 12,000 seat domed stadium that was the largest of its kind in the United States, at the time. Many prominent acts would go on to play the Coliseum throughout the 1950s and '60s, up to the present day. Another popular place for large shows was the Park Center, which hosted everything from country music shows to Motown revues, with Rock & Roll shows highlighted sporadically. Much smaller venues were also around throughout Mecklenburg County, and the surrounding towns.*

ROB THORNE: Most of the bands that played were like square-dance bands. All the hot spots for that kind of activities were American Legion Posts, and stuff like that. There was one out on Highway 16, going out toward the lake that was an American Legion Post. Dicky Dixon and The Loafers, that were real a popular kind of a Rockabilly band, played out there all of the time. And they would do the popular music of the day, they would do country, kind of Rockabilly stuff, and then they'd do a square-dance set. It was a kind of a mixture of stuff in those type venues. There weren't many live music clubs. Not like now. And not like there were later in the Sixties. In the early Sixties, when I first got with the Catalinas, there was a place called The B&G Trading Post, which was on South Boulevard where Paul's Lounge was, later on.

In Charlotte, the music scene was kind of polarized. If you grew up on the west side and hung on the west side, that's where you did most of what you did. People on the east side might have had another place to go to although I can't tell you what was over there on the east side, I don't remember on the east side other than The Tree House when it first opened up over on Independence Boulevard. The B&G Trading Post, like I said, was one over on South Boulevard. Mickey's Lounge was on Morehead Street.

Now, they didn't use bands like the Catalinas. They used lounge bands. There were a lot of loungey kind of things going on in town. With lounge bands that played a slightly different style and didn't play the same things as the Catalinas, or the Rivieras or some of what the white soul bands played. It was a whole different thing for some reason, I don't know why. I think there might have been a country place or two that was strictly Country. But see, most of the private clubs like the Elks Club or the Moose club or Am Vets, used that kind of bands that played a variety of country, Poppy, square-dancey stuff.

DANIEL COSTON: *Another musical genre that began to take shape in the late 1950s was folk music. On the surface, folk music seemed a lot tamer than Rock & Roll. Much of the folk music stars of the 1950s were clean-cut college kids, singing in a group style that owed more to the Four Freshmen than Elvis Presley. However, American folk music shared some of the same multi-race influence as Rock & Roll, and could talk about subjects, such as equality, poverty, human rights and politics, that Rock & Roll would not touch until the late 1960s. During that time, folk music would change, and would continue to influence what one could say in a pop song. Many in Charlotte would also take an interest in folk music, and find their way into various venues.*

ROB THORNE: There was a place downtown called The El Greco, which was a coffeehouse above Tanner's Snack Bar, across from the Library. It's where Discovery Place is now.

It was called El Greco for a while, and then it was called Zanadu. And Nick Stravakis owned it. It was kind of beatnik/hippie-ish, the beginning of Hippie and the tail end of Beatnik in the early 60's when folk music was really hot. They would have jug bands, individuals, duos, groups. I would go down there and play a washtub bass, and I'm not a bass player but I can make one thump. It was a lot of fun to do that. That's where I met Jon Mullis and Lee Stewart, and some people like that, that were really big in that folk scene at the time.

There was a girl named Mary Ann Hayberg. She was a beautiful, blonde Norwegian girl who lived here, folksinger, and she went to Boston and disappeared from the scene. There were a lot of girl guitar players playing folky kind of things because it was real popular, and they all looked great, they all had that same kind of "look" that the guys were crazy about.

DAVE LONG: There was a place across from the library called the Zanadu Coffeehouse. It was upstairs, and Jack Pennington did the inside in a Turkish motif. I would see Jon Mullis there, about 1965. A guy named Dave Watson played there, too. Great player. Don't forget the folk stuff. John Moss. Larry Head. Jon was an original guy. He got me into the folk music scene. He was ahead of the singer-songwriter curve. Back then, you either played an electric guitar, or you were a folk guy.

SHORTY NEHRENBERG: I guess it was the country-blues, like the John Hammond country blues, sounded like something we'd never heard before, and you tried to kind of imitate those kind of sounds, I guess. Because that's where it all started from, there wasn't any real Rock & Roll. There was folk music and blues, and trying to find some way to make them sound relevant or good.

And then, like, to learn a song, you know, you're trying to tune up with a record that was record off a tape that's never in tune, and the only thing we had were pitch pipes. There were no tuners, and so you're sitting there trying to figure a song out, it takes you forever, whereas nowadays you can learn one in like three minutes!

So we would hear about a band, or some kind of music. And we'd go to a music store and of course it wasn't there. There was no such thing. They certainly didn't stock the kind of music we liked. So my friend Dennis Edwards would hear about it, or I'd hear about it, you'd read about something in Folkways Magazine or something, and we'd go to Ernie's Records Shop, and get Ernie to order some of this stuff that we'd heard about for us. And then a couple of weeks later we'd actually get the record.

collection of Shorty Nehrenberg

Shorty Nehrenberg, 1967.

You'd hear a song on a record at a friend's house and you wouldn't hear it again for a year, unless you were lucky enough to get that record! So, it's not like nowadays when anything there is, is available to everybody. So you'd hear something on the radio and stop your car to listen to it. So everybody was tuned in to finding the music and enjoying the music and gathering it together. And Ernie's Records would start stocking stuff in his store and wait for us to come in and get it after a while. And eventually we saw more of it around, but it wasn't that accessible at first. The people around here were listening to the older stuff, and there was a real generation gap. We weren't listening to any of that, and the world was just changing to being more in tune to the young people, at that time. Before then, in my parents' generation, the world was centered around them. Nowadays it's centered around kids, and we were the first wave of that. Kids with money and time, and disposable income.

ROB THORNE: There were a lot of jazz clubs at the time. There were more jazz clubs than anything else. Across from Nicky's, on Morehead Street, where the Center Theatre was, was a place called the Blue Note Lounge. They had great jazz down there on the weekends and Folk Music on Sunday nights. And every now and then on a Sunday they'd bring in somebody like The Catalinas, or a band like that. There was a place out on Wilkinson Boulevard called The Lodge. That was a great jazz club. There was also a club, and I'm not sure if it was a restaurant, supper-club kind of place, The El Morocco Supper Club.

Most of the guys in the Catalinas had that quality of musicianship already under their belts by the time they were kids, they could all play like hell! It was unbelievable. I've never seen so many young people play so well. It's not like that now. And it hasn't been like that in a long time. During the 70's, and times like that. During the psychedelic period, when most of these guys were coming up. Unfortunately, a lot of those musicians, and some that I'd known and had played with, copped an attitude that all they were going to play psychedelic Rock & Roll. They weren't gonna play any of this other stuff that they considered to be beneath them. And so a lot of them missed the boat on broadening their foundation, and having a huge foundation to build on so that they could work with anybody that came down the pike. And be able to do sessions and really broaden their musical horizons. The attitude at the time may have been tied to drugs as well, during that time period. And it limited a lot of those guys from learning more than they could have. But my generation, in the early sixties, man, we never would have thought that. We just wanted to play anything. Didn't matter what it was. Anytime. Anywhere.

DANIEL COSTON: *By the late 1950s, Rock & Roll had been declared dead for the first time in its history. The stars of that first wave had been waylaid by scandal, tragic plane and car accidents, and record labels that suddenly thought that Rock & Roll was a thing of the past. Elvis Presley was drafted by the US Army, and then by Hollywood. Safe teen idols took his place. But, as it often happens, the spirit of Rock & Roll went elsewhere. Into the garages of young instrumental groups, hoping that the single that they had paid for, and released themselves would find a larger audience. To California, where sounds ranging from the surf guitar Rock of Dick Dale, to the Rock, Doo-Wop and vocal harmony sounds of Jan & Dean, and the Beach Boys. Rock & Roll also went overseas during this time, and would re-emerge on our shores in just a few years.*

Meanwhile, back in North Carolina, a new genre began to emerge. Rhythm & Blues, and the music of the emerging Motown record label, in a hybrid that owed more to the early soul records of James Brown. The music was danceable, and predominantly white audiences discovered it during trips to Myrtle Beach, SC, or the Outer Banks of North Carolina. Given its proximity to the beach, the music became known as "Beach Music," although many of the first wave of musicians were based throughout North Carolina, including Charlotte.

BARRY STACKS: The bands back home were two guitars, bass and drums. If someone could sing, you'd rehearse a few songs. There was no such thing as a PA in those days, so if the place you were playing had some sort of microphone system set up, you'd do a couple of those numbers. When I got to Charlotte, I went to Myers Park High School, and I met a guy named Dave Efird, and he played with a band called Sonny and the Sunliners. He called it "a little outfit", and they rehearsed about a block from my house. One day, I went to see what all this noise was. They had a couple of trumpets, a sax, a trombone player, a guitarist, a bass player, and three backup singers! Later on, Dave took me to see a group called Bob Meyer and the Rivieras, and they had pretty much the same set-up. They had a horn section, and they did stuff by James Brown, as did the Sunliners. None of these musicians were self-taught. They had all taken lessons on the instruments that they played. It was a completely different music scene. Dave also took me to see the Tams, and these guys just blew me away.

DANIEL COSTON: *Many of the top groups of the genre's first and second wave came from North Carolina. This includes the Catalinas, the Tassels, Billy Scott, Gene Barbour and the Cavaliers, Harry Deal and the Galaxies, and the Embers. The O'Kaysions, from Wilson, saw their song "Girl Watcher" reach the Top 10 in 1968, while the Spontanes saw their song "Where Did I Go Wrong?" released nationally by United Artists Records that same year. Charlotte's own Tempests released an album on the Smash Mercury label in 1968. Still more beach groups recorded and released their own albums during the 1960s, and sold them at their shows.*

ROB THORNE: As a sixteen to seventeen year old kid, playing with The Catalinas or a band that was like that that was extremely popular, we traveled the same circuit, or places like the Park Center, places like that. And the shows usually consisted of one or two opening acts that were white, and then the rest of the show was loaded down with recording acts that were black.

Well, we played with those people on these shows, we even backed up a lot of those girls. The Catalinas did, because we had a rhythm section that could play and read or understand the arrangements and stuff like that. And we emulated the black players. We'd stand along the side at the edge of the stage at the Park Center, or any other venues like that that we played while these professionals were playing, and man, we were just soaking it up, watching these guys, I was always just glued to the drummers. And everybody in the band was watching the guitar player, or the bass player or the piano player. Or the singers were watching the singers up front, to get the groove, to just get a taste of what was going on. And it was a real learning experience for us to watch these people. But honestly, by the time I got with the Catalinas, those guys were as professional as any of the bands that they were on tour with. They'd already been doing it since 1957. And I got there in '60, or '61. They could sing, they could dance, they didn't have a horn section though, but they had a great drummer! I replaced a drummer named Mark Alexander who could play at that time like Buddy Rich!

So, the quality was there already in these white kids. But we wanted to sound like a black band. So we tried everything we could just to sound like a black soul band. Down to the Doo-Woppy voices and the instrumentation and the big thumping bass and the grooves that we played on the drums. And most of the bands that were popular at that time were like that, like the Catalinas, or the Rivieras. There were probably six or eight really good bands that did openers on all these shows that had that sound. That almost approached that black groove sound.

Then there was another level of white bands that would play on those shows also, that had a more loungey kind of feel. Even though it was the same music, it was not as groovy. They didn't understand the arrangements. And a lot of them couldn't play the proper chords the way they were supposed to be.

The beach music that is being played now and that has been played for the past forty years or so, I guess from the late Sixties on out, the white bands have made it even more white and took it away from the kind of black groove that we were tying to emulate, for some reason. I don't know why that happened. I guess that maybe a lot of the bands that are carrying the banner now may have had kind of a lounge kind of attitude, kind of a lounge groove attitude.

And I like a lot of those bands. The groups like the Embers kind of lightened it all up a little bit when they came along, I think. They put that more loungey kind of feel to it. And I don't think they really had that hard-core black groove. And a lot of bands took their leads from the Embers because they were extremely popular in the Seventies. I mean they were working more than probably anybody. They were making more money than anybody. And they kind of set the tone for Beach, at that time. And that's why I don't like that term and I don't like that approach to it. I like it hard and sweating. That's the way R&B is supposed to be. Especially after watching the black guys do it. They would do it to death. God, it was unbelievable! But, that's Beach Music now.

DANIEL COSTON: *By late 1963, America was ready for a change, even if it didn't know it. The country reeled from the assassination of president John F. Kennedy in the November of that year. Civil rights unrest had highlighted the entire year. A new generation was restless for something different, something that they could call their own. That would arrive in a matter of weeks.*

JAKE BERGER: Before the Beatles played [Ed Sullivan], every Eckerd's had these displays that would have the Meet The Beatles LP cover with their faces blocked out, and they would say, "The Beatles are coming."

1964, First Bands and First Gigs

JAKE BERGER: For most of my contemporaries, our musical awareness and interest arrived on the same jet that brought the Beatles to our shores. And in a sense, me, too. I had shown a little interest in pop music, but as a pre-teen, it wasn't a driving force in my life. I was closing in on my teenage years when the Fabs made their appearance, and remember well all the fuss prior to the performance. One of my pals named Jimmy Glasgow had an older sister who was all agog at the impending performance. I saw the actual show at my step-cousin's house. I don't remember it making a huge impression on me, and neither did the following week's performance. Then the floodgate of English bands spewed forth all kinds of hair shaking precocious "lads" with their North England accents, and I got caught up in the mania like everybody else.

My other bud who lived across the road from me, Brad Smith, was an artistic kind of kid who later became a truck driver and biker, had formed with his next door neighbor a little pantomime group with fake guitars and I, for lack of anything better to do, became part of the "Beatle Juniors". I was eleven at the time. Later that summer, we all went to the Family Dollar store and bought, for $3 apiece, three identical work-able plastic guitars, and set about doing, well, not much.

It would take another few months, and Brad's exclamation that "Their hair is down to here!" to get me fired up about a band that hadn't even played on our shores yet. After a short interval of "summer camp", I returned home and saw on the Evening News a little blurb about some new English band that had started a riot in Scotland when the guitarist had kicked someone in the front row in the head. This was something that an entertainer in a Rock & Roll band wouldn't normally do. At that time, the English bands that had slipped in the door with the Beatles were "nice" boys! That band was slated for Ed Sullivan the very next week!

It's pointless to go on and on about the anticipation while waiting for that week to go by. When Sunday night rolled around, I was primed and ready, and this is where it all started for me. The curtains opened, and five guys that you just knew were up to the same kind of no good that you wished you could be up to, ambled forward. "Well the joint was a rocking, goin' 'round and 'round", followed by the nastiest, blackest sounding, just plain bad-assed, "Ti-yi-ee-yime, is on my side", and the Rolling Stones entered my life. These are the guys that introduced about every white kid of my age group to the awesome musical art form that had sprung from the black community known as R&B, and from there morphed into Soul music. To me it seemed to come from nowhere, but in reality had evolved from the first completely original American art form, jazz, in the late 1800's. It came out of the south in the form of Ragtime and Dixieland jazz, splintered and from one offshoot became delta blues, made the northern migration to Detroit and notably Chicago, became urban blues, stayed in the south and became Rhythm & Blues. From there it was copied by whites in the south, and became R&B's weaker cousin Rock & Roll, and then as it got more watered down, it all but died until our British cousins brought it all back home.

DANIEL COSTON: *In 1956, much of England's youth was swept up by the Skiffle craze. Skiffle music was a mixture of American folk music and traditional jazz. Skiffle was easy to play, whether you were playing guitar, banjo, washboard bass, or drums, if one could afford them. Kids like John Lennon formed their own band to play Skiffle, but were soon swayed by the Rock & Roll sounds they were hearing from America.*

Records from America were often hard to come by. Some were brought to England by sailors who were docked in seaport towns such as Liverpool, where Lennon and the soon-to-be Beatles grew up. Others were attained third-hand from stores that imported, or re-produced these albums for collectors. Many listeners throughout Europe did not divide up the American music that they were hearing. Blues, folk, Rock & Roll, country, R&B, Motown. To the rest of the world, it was all American music, and the new listeners soaked it up.

Soon, many of these kids were playing the music that they were listening to. Bands such as the Beatles showed a love of early Rock records, as well as R&B and Motown. Others were taken up by American blues music. By the early 1960s, many American musicians began touring regularly across Europe. This gave many of the young English bands the chance to open for, play with and occasionally record with their heroes. It also gave many of these groups the confidence to push their music beyond England. Maybe America wasn't so out of reach, after all?

Would the British Invasion have happened without the Beatles? Possibly, but certainly not with the impact that the Beatles had in the early months of 1964. Just a few months before, Beatles manager Brian Epstein had secured the band an appearance on the Ed Sullivan TV show without benefit of a hit single in the U.S., or even before Capitol Records had committed to releasing and promoting the next Beatles single. When "I Want To Hold Your Hand" went to number one the week before the Sullivan appearance, it seemed that all the stars were lining up for the Beatles, and the United States. The revolution was about to be televised.

BOYD ALBRITTON: A friend of mine said, "Hey man, check this out. There's this band in England that people are going crazy over, and they're gonna show it on Ed Sullivan."

DAVE LONG: It just exploded. Everybody was waiting for them to be on.

BOBBY DONALDSON: I remember the Life Magazine when the Beatles came out, and the lighting in the magazine made them all look like they had red hair.

DOUG JAMES: It was the Beatles and The Rolling Stones and that sort of stuff that captivated me, and I just started using my paper route money to buy instruments like guitars and basses, and building amplifiers out of Hi-Fi's. Just whatever it took.

BARRY STACKS: By 1964, I was eighteen. I had moved out of my father's house, and was living near his shop, where I worked during the day. In February of that year, the Beatles showed up on TV. I was sitting with my friend Bob Crawford, and we looked at each other, and said, "That's it, right there. Nobody around here is going to have the balls to do that." Let their hair grow long, all of that. We were the only band in Charlotte that was doing that in Charlotte, when we started. Although the Beatles did blow me away, it wasn't until I heard the Kinks that I knew we were on to something. That we were going in the right direction. Because we were raunchy, like the Kinks were.

PAT WALTERS: I was about eleven years old when The Beatles hit the United States. Through my teenage sisters, I listened to Rock & Roll, and Rhythm & Blues kind of stuff that was out on the radio. I was into it, but I didn't play anything. I wanted to. So when the Beatles and all the British Invasion bands came out, I said, "Okay, I must have a guitar. I must learn to play the guitar and get in a band." And that was the beginning.

JAKE BERGER: The two local radio AM stations that were white-oriented, WIST and WAYS, very quickly upped their game during 1964, and it's during that time period that I still think to this day is when radio was at it's peak. There was at that time no segregation in their formats. I remember distinctly listening one night, instead of doing homework, and the playlist was something along these lines. "Wooly Bully" by Sam the Sham & The Pharoahs, followed by "Baby's in Black" by the Beatles, and into "The Race Is On" by George Jones, capped off by the Stones' version of "Little Red Rooster". Interspersed between the "new" longhaired white kid bands that were playing their own version of black American music were also American artists of color, now in the forefront of what had till this point been the domain of "white kid" oriented material. This is when I heard for the first time the artists that originated the music that I first heard performed by the British artists. Wonderful new sounds by all the Motown greats. Marvin Gaye, Junior Walker, the "Tempting" Temptations, and even more appealing, the southern soul artists. The Tams, Don Covay, Wilson Pickett, and of course all the Stax music, with Booker T. & The MG's, and Otis Redding.

ROB THORNE: When I saw the Beatles that first time, it ruined me. I still loved R&B and stuff like that, but it piqued my interest and I wanted to play that kind of music, that kind of music. Like I said, I loved playing R&B music, but it was an easy transition to move into that and to play Blues Rock kind of stuff, also, because I had that R&B background real solid on the bottom end kind of feel.

STEVE STOECKEL: A lot of the older musicians didn't like the Beatles because they couldn't see the musical value in it, to be honest. And to be fair, if you heard those early singles, "Love Me Do" and such, musically it wasn't top form. They hadn't gotten to the intricate stuff. If you had been playing soul music, or intricate playing that required a lot of musical chops, you heard the first Beatles record, you'd be going, "These guys are amateurs." You wouldn't have heard the harmonies. You wouldn't see the potential. You wouldn't have been caught up in the visual impact.

ROB THORNE: I thought that The Stones were really amateurish, and I actually thought that they were terrible! And they were at first! It wasn't very good! And I was trained enough and experienced enough to know the difference between someone who had studied or tried to learn and play up to a certain level and the bands that were not so good.

The problem at that time was, up until that time most of the musicians who were on records were really good musicians, even if it was just poppy stuff. There was enough foundation and training, because a lot of them were studio musicians who did the backup music, but still it was fine playing. And when The Stones and all those type people came on, they couldn't play that well, but it sold. It didn't matter. The record labels realized that they could market amateurs and get away with it. That changed with people like Hendrix and Cream, and the bands like that who were really hardcore and could really play during that period. I liked that stuff.

The Invasion stuff kind of left me a little cold. Except for The Beatles. They were The One. They were the main one. They were the ones that I think were the better of all those groups that had that poppy kind of feel in that Invasion stuff. That's what set them apart. But the Beatles really dug into that stuff and almost from the mid-Fifties on, all of that stuff that came over to them on records that they were listening to, like Elvis, and Little

Richard. They would really lock in to that sort of stuff. And it really showed in their earlier records. Of course, "I Wanna Hold Your Hand" was just a knockout the first time I saw and heard it! I thought, "Man, this is just unbelievable stuff!" That altered my whole look. All of a sudden I wasn't "Mr. College Guy". I let my hair grow and I grew a beard, and I think I got my ears pierced! I just went to hell, as far as they were concerned.

LARRY DUCKWORTH: I had been in Judo, and Jimmy [Duckworth] was, too. We had done very well with that. I had been four times state champion. Couldn't meet a girl to save my life! I mean, it would stink! I mean, we wanted to grow our hair long, but they were all uppity about long hair in the Judo thing, and I did all this stuff and maybe I met one girl, one time.

I'd been up at my cousin's house, and he had a drum set, and I heard this album by the Ventures. Well, I'd been playing accordion and I was in the school band since I was seven, so I just sat down and said, "Well, this isn't that bad! I can do that!" I had some friends who had a band, and their drummer had a great drum set, but he couldn't play "Wipe Out". So, they would let me sit in for the one tune. Well, next thing I know, I'm talking to girls! I thought, "This rocks!" All I need is a tom-tom and I'm good to go! So, I got a tom-tom and they kicked that guy out and I was in, because I could play the other tunes as well, and then I played this one party, and I ended up talking to a whole lot of girls! And I thought, "This is the stuff! This is what I wanna do!"

RONNIE PHILLIPS: I started by playing guitar. We would take a Ventures album, play a bit of it, stop the record, learn the part, and play the rest of the record. But when I started playing drums, I knew that's what I wanted to do.

DOUG JAMES: It was the Beatles and the Rolling Stones and that sort of stuff that captivated me, and I just started using my paper route money to buy instruments like guitars and basses, and building amplifiers out of Hi-Fi's, just whatever it took. And that's really all I've ever done since then.

DAVID FLOYD: When I got to be in seventh grade, I bought, I think it was the Beatles, and then I wanted to get into combos. Do you remember those organs that were called, Magnus Chord Organs? I bought that first. And it had these buttons down here that you'd press to make chords. And somehow I miked that thing and got it to go through a PA system and I could play with my guitar-playing friends. I never took any lessons for playing keyboards, but I could play chords over there, and I'd do that and try to figure out the notes that made the same sounds, and that's how I learned how to play keyboards.

photo by Barbara Carter, courtesy of Vicki Surrett Graham

The Sinclairs, Veteran's Park, 1964.

BOBBY DONALDSON: I never made a decision to say, "This is what I want to do." I just kept doing it. I do remember standing at the Park Center, and hearing Curtis Mayfield playing guitar with the Impressions. The sound that was coming off the stage, I think something just clicked in me.

DANIEL COSTON: *As soon as the Beatles conquered America, it seemed that hundreds of British bands suddenly appeared, ready to follow their path to success. For every new Beatles single, there were songs by the Kinks, Dave Clark Five, Herman's Hermits, Searchers, Freddy and the Dreamers, Gerry and the Pacemakers, the Rolling Stones, Yardbirds, Animals, Zombies, Chad & Jeremy, Peter & Gordon, and Petula Clark, among many others. Soon, kids across the country were forming their own bands, and starting their own careers in music. Charlotte was no different, with kids such as Pat Walters joining his first band for his very first show.*

PAT WALTERS: There was a little group called the Sinclairs. I think we were named after a gas station. That was in seventh grade. We actually won the talent show at Eastway. Steve Stoeckel can remember, to this day, seeing me playing on top of the dugout with the Sinclairs. John Bolick was in the Sinclairs. Dave Brakefield was the drummer.

STEVE STOECKEL: We all wanted to be the Beatles. We wanted to meet girls. You look at pictures of me and Pat Walters back then, it was the only prayer we had. None of us were going to be on the basketball team. We just huddled up in bedrooms and garages, and learned to play this stuff.

The first time it occurred to me was at a draw for a talent show at Eastway Junior High. The paper said, "The Sinclairs will be playing on the dugout of the baseball field of Eastway Junior High," and it was Pat and three other guys. I wasn't playing in a band at this time. I was just playing by myself. They played "Twist and Shout," and they sounded wonderful. It was the first band I had heard live. I looked around, and all the girls were staring at them. And I thought, "This is what I need to be doing." Within a couple of months, I was in a band. Any male during that time would by lying if they didn't say that they got into being in a band to get girls, and be the Beatles.

PAT WALTERS: We didn't have a bass player. It was just like John was there some and he was not there some, so we had a guy who played tambourine. You remember the old silver Christmas trees? They had a stand with the piece of wood painted silver. So I commandeered that from my house and we had a little $2 microphone that I taped on. It was terrible. Terrible stuff! I don't know how we got up there, but somebody got us up there.

We played at a talent show over at Midwood Elementary School, over on Central Avenue. That might have been the very first gig. I remember thinking, "Oh, stage fright, how do I get over that?" and I remember reading about some star who just looked at the clock at the back of the auditorium. So that's what I did! I didn't have any trouble after that.

KEN KNIGHT: I had been messing some with six-string guitars. One day, in history class, I saw these other guys, and we were all talking about guitars. They said, "Do you play bass?" And I said yes, and I didn't play bass at all. So I went home, and my dad helped me get a bass. I went to the audition two days later, and I played "For Your Love," by the Yardbirds. They had just had somebody pick out the low notes on a guitar before me, and when I could play the middle part of the song, I had the job.

TIM TATUM: I think the British invasion had a big part of us getting into playing. That being said, we were one of the few white kids that would go out and see the Motown revues at Park Center. There'd be twelve acts on the bill. Jackie Wilson would be the headliner. We were into a lot of music. The music was just so pure, at that time.

KEN KNIGHT: I hadn't been in the band very long, and we got this gig, and I didn't know all of the songs yet. I asked, "What do I do?" And Tommy said, "Just turn your amp off and play along." You should have seen me working the neck of that bass!

DONNY FLETCHER: When we started out, we were the only band in Cramerton. Before that, in about eighth grade, we would pantomime at these parties. We'd pick some records. I had a little set of cocktail set of drums. The rest of the band would borrow guitars. My best memory of that is at this party. They always had the drummers on drum risers, so they put the drums on this serving tray that had castor wheels on the bottom. So they somehow got a curtain set up, and all of our friends were there. So they put the first record on, and they pushed me out on stage. I remember thinking, "I'm about to fall off of this thing!"

BARRY STACKS: The Beatles' set-up, two guitars players, a bass player and a drummer, that's what the Galaxies had. I had done some singing with the Galaxies, and I had met this guy from Kershaw, SC named Bob Crawford while living at the boarding house. We started playing together. We eventually decided that we were driving everybody nuts at the boarding house, so we rented a house together. We heard about another guitar player named Mike Wingate, and we went through a couple of drummers before we found Roy Skinner.

ROY SKINNER: I was playing drums in High School, and someone said to me, "I've been playing with these guys, but I can't do it anymore. You should try out for them." So I auditioned, and got the job.

BARRY STACKS: We went into the studio about eighteen months before we did the recording for "Catch A Ride". Somebody said, "I'd like to record you guys." There were a couple of clubs that were popping up, on Tryon Street. There were a couple of clubs popping up, and we got into that, and Bobby and I had decided that we were going to do as much writing as we could. We were going to write our own music. Everything that seemed to be coming out of England was original music. We recorded out at Arthur Smith [in 1964], and realized that we weren't good enough, yet, to do any recording. So we waited until 1965.

1965 and 1966

JAKE BERGER: Every fall in Charlotte there is an "arts festival" aptly named The Festival In The Park, because it is held in Freedom Park. In the early and mid Sixties, it was a weeklong event held with some anticipation by the locals, and most of all, by the kids. That was a place that kids were allowed to go without parental supervision, and we all made the most of it. We ran hog-assed wild!

Back in the day, there was no Main Stage, and beat groups were sparse, at best. There was always a folk music tent, and I witnessed several good folkies then, but occasionally there would be a tent with an actual combo playing. The first ever live band I saw in Charlotte was there. I remember as if it were yesterday. Walking down the hill (which would later become infamous in its own right), and watching as a small group of kids started assembling "The Gear"! I cannot tell you how exciting that was for me. I was infatuated by everything that had the slightest connection to beat music, and I could look for hours at magazines containing all the latest on the English, and by this time American bands. Checking out the clothes, the gear, and the look. So when the Twi-lighters, as they turned out to be, cranked it up, I was over the moon. It didn't matter to me in the least that they had no vocalist. I thought they were fabulous. In retrospect, I think they were made up of three older guys, college aged, and one teenager on the drums. They played "Love Potion #9" and "Mr. Tambourine Man". Both songs had just entered the American charts. This was 1965, and the heat was on!

That same night, I went over the bridge that crosses Sugar Creek and over to the Charlotte Nature Museum, where there was another combo just starting to play. They were not dressed to the nines in the latest, and their gear looked suspect, with the little guy on guitar sporting the same model "Woolworth's Royal" guitar that I had been slobbering over at Park Road Shopping Center for a few months ($29, back then). They were the Abbadons, from Charlotte, and they were about as a non-Rock & Roll looking band as you would hope to see, except for the tall one that had dyed his sneakers purple. All I remember is that they played "Wipe Out" more than a few times, had no singer and were probably the first taste, but not the last, of live garage band music, which would in the near future become a genre all it's own. Years later, I found out while researching for this book that the Abbadons had most certainly played there and had most certainly not obtained permission.

But since it was their stomping ground, they had decided to play The Festival In The Park". Classic! They were not to be the last ensemble that I would be exposed to at the festival.

The following evening, I saw a very professional group called the Greystones. This group featured the already exceptional guitarist, Bobby Donaldson, and another scary good guitarist, Robert Fallows. They did an Arthur Alexander tune called "You Better Move On" that the Rolling Stones had covered two years before. (The Beatles had covered another Alexander song, "Anna", on their first LP). The Greystones were an eye opener for me, all the "wild" gyrations and guitar acrobatics like playing behind the head and between the legs that Jimi Hendrix astounded the world with years later, were on display that night by that little group of Junior High school kids. What I didn't know was that the sort of crazed guitar and stage play, complete with sexual connotations had been a staple of the older, professional, black Rhythm & Blues bands for decades. Those very first music groups have stayed in my memory as fresh as if it happened today, and I will always count these and subsequent performances by the Abbadons and bands that included Bobby Donaldson as not only pure musical enjoyment, but also musical instruction. I watched and I learned every time I could manage to see a real live band.

In an age where the song doesn't sell the band, the image does via video, where nearly every kid on the planet owns an expensive instrument and believes fervently that he or she is destined to "be a star", and where your idols are manufactured by Walt at Disneyworld, it's very hard to wrap your head around the vision of teenagers framming out dumb, uncomplicated power chords on the cheapest of the cheap guitars and rickety old amplifiers in their dad's garage. The fact that some actually did put out their own records, which in itself was a feat, all done without the internet, without American Idol, and completely done as a "do it yourself" project done solely for fun and excitement. As I remind myself, it's a different world, but I'm sorry for all the lost wonder of discovering something so unique, of a decade of musical innovation, of sometimes bizarre musical deviations. Despite still being less than ten years old at that time, Rock & Roll stretched the imagination and stretched musical and social boundaries. It was all really only there for five or six years, and now is gone, never to be repeated.

DANIEL COSTON: *While 1964 was year zero for the cultural explosion of the entire decade, in my opinion 1965 and 1966 is the period where the music really began to go from black & white, to full-blown technicolor. New ideas, new music everywhere. Really good music, everywhere.*

At the beginning of 1965, British bands were still ruling the U.S. charts, but there were rumblings of an American counter-attacks. Bands like the Byrds, Beau Brummels, and others began to climb the charts. Bob Dylan had started the year as the poet laureate of folk music, but soon began to have other ideas. When Dylan stepped on the Newport Folk Festival stage that June with an electric guitar, playing his newly released "Like A Rolling Stone," there was no going back for folk, or Rock music. The music and ideas were beginning to move faster than the mainstream was sometimes prepared for, but budding musicians in Charlotte, and elsewhere continued to take it all in, and make it their own.

ZAN MCLEOD: I met this young guy named Danny Fellows. He was my age, but in those days we was a little tiny guy. He looked like he was a little kid, and he weighed about 80 pounds and he was about 5'1", and he could play just unbelievably well, he would just freak people out! He had the ability to hear solos, like Jimi Hendrix or Eric Clapton. His nickname was Munk, and Munk had flaming red hair, and the solos like Jim Hendrix or Clapton, he could copy exactly! I mean, exactly! He could memorize it in, like 15 minutes. He could play like Hendrix, before anyone around here could play like Hendrix. He could play all those chords. I learned all that stuff from him.

Munk's brother was a really good guitar player, too. He got killed in Vietnam. Robert. I even went to Robert's funeral. I remember that. I recently found my draft card! I almost got drafted! Yeah, I got close.

I didn't really own a guitar until the other neighbor we had, the neighbor on the other side of Fred Kirby's house, had two guitars. He knew we wanted a guitar, and he had a Kay Acoustic that he sold to my dad really cheap. So the first guitar that I had was around 1966.

BOYD ALBRITTON: Early on, I was the bass player, and I would play on one string. I was just learning how to play. Later, I paid $80 to Melvin Cohen for a little amp. My first guitar was a Kay guitar. I was a big nut for the Who, and the Kinks. I could play the Temptations, and all that other stuff like that, but it wasn't my thing. I won't knock that music, though. That came in handy with Buddy Miles, years later. That's how I got that gig with him.

DANIEL COSTON: *Other aspiring musicians were finding other ways of getting hold of a guitar.*

BOBBY DONALDSON: I built my first guitar in shop class, in school! The other kids were making bookends, and I was making a guitar. And it worked. It had to work! It was the only guitar I had! We were so excited to get out and play, I didn't worry about other bands. Unless you were in a Battle Of The Bands, you were playing in one place, and everyone else was playing another. I was always the baby in bands.

JAKE BERGER: I went to Cochrane Junior High for the summer, where I met Jim Lindsey. His story, which was later corroborated by his mom, was that he had run away from their home in High Point, NC, and ended up on the streets of Greenwich Village, in New York. This was pretty impressive to me. You have to keep in mind this had happened in late 1965, and Jim was 14 years old. All summer, I would go to his home and skip summer school with him. All day, we would listen to music. Jim's mom hated me, and blamed his bad attitude on me. I found out later that she blamed all of his pals for his shortcomings. Once, Pat Walters was napping at home after school, when in blasts Jim's mom and proceeds to grill Pat as to where Jim was, blaming him all the while for leading her baby astray!

The very first combo that I ever attempted to make music with (after the Beatle Juniors, of course) was with Jim playing bass on his dad's guitar, a fellow named Nelson Morris on drums, and Ronnie Smith, a friend from my street, on guitar. I was the "front guy", singing as best I could, and beating a tambourine like it owed me money! That group of guys lasted about three weeks.

I really didn't start going out and playing guitar until late 1966. My first electric guitar was a Kay guitar, a cheap thing, about $35. I got it at Reliable Pawn Shop. I'd gotten my first acoustic guitar the year before. It was a Silvertone. Roses had them, Eckerd's had them. There was the pawn shops. There was a Tillman's Music, a big store on East Independence, which became Howren, later. Sustar's Music Store was the first free-standing store. Sustar's had a store uptown, which he later moved down to Elizabeth Avenue. I was just a kid, and before I could afford a guitar, Larry used to let me come in there every day and come in and play. He was a nice guy, and he encouraged me. I ended buying a black face Fender Bassman from him for $200.

DANIEL COSTON: *In early 1965, Pat Walters had joined up with the Barons, and began playing more throughout the Carolinas.*

PAT WALTERS: Those guys were like a year or more older than me. They were listening to The Stones and The Pretty Things. They were so sure of themselves, too, and really, they had been playing less time than me, but they were like, "Oh yeah, we got gigs and we got an agent." and I thought, "Man! In six months I'm gonna have a new

The Barons, 1966.

Vox amplifier and be a star!" Yeah, they had a lot of spunk, and they were fun guys to hang out with.

Some of them went to school at Eastway, and it was like there were three other long-haired guys, then. They didn't want to acknowledge me too much, and I didn't want to acknowledge them. But it was cool, and I thought, "They're not jocks! They've got long hair and they're not jocks!" So I met them, and I kind of knew Tim Moore because he lived near me. I'd been to see "Help!" and they were coming out of the theater, and it was like, "Hey! Do you wanna join our band, the Barons? We've got an audition in about a week, man!" So, I said, "Sure, I'll check it out."

Hit Attractions was run by an agent named Ted Hall. Somehow, someone knew somebody who knew Ted Hall, and he said, "Okay, send your guys over." There was a dance studio, up on Emerywood, and I think there is some other kind of business in there now. Phil Lowe reminded me that they had all the bands set up in the parking lot. And that's what we did.

I remember a great black band, that was like a guy had a Telecaster with a strap around the wrong shoulder and it was all beat up, with cigarette burns everywhere. And doing the funkiest, most soulful stuff, and I thought, "Good God, it'd be neat to sound sort of like that some day." But, based on that, Hit Attractions did get us some gigs, like opening for Herman's Hermits, and it has got to be just because we were just little Mod kids.

We couldn't keep a bass player, and Karl Jarvi came and played with us. He was like five years older than the rest of us, or at least that much older than me. We were in school, we couldn't drive. We still were friends. Karl started playing with a band that Steve Stoeckel was a rhythm guitar player in, T.C. Atlantic. The drummer for T.C. Atlantic was David Brakefield, formerly of The Sinclairs.

JAKE BERGER: The only time I saw the Barons took place during the summer of 1966. This was in-between a short lived try at forming a group with Jim Lindsey, Nelson Morris and Ronnie Smith, who lived near me, and actually forming a band later that year with Ronnie, Doug James and Gary Plavidal. Ronnie asked if I wanted to go to the Soapbox Derby, which was being held on Tyvola Road. We only wanted to go because Ronnie had heard there was going to be a band playing. At that time and at that age, seeing a live band was not something you would look in the Entertainment section of the paper, and easily find.

When the Barons made their appearance, they just knocked us out. They were a scruffy bunch with hair that was way too long for conventions. The music that they played was aggressive, and very Stones-ish in delivery. I remember a very good "I'm A Man", a la Yardbirds, but something else I saw that was a phonemenom that was just starting to become a regular occurrence. Long hair was on the cusp of changing over from a cute "Beatle-like" image, to something more subversive. This attitude was in part enhanced by the anti-establishment image of groups like the Rolling Stones and the Pretty Things, and now being adopted by youth worldwide. There was of course a backlash coming, but at this time it would take the guise of harmless, and not so harmless teasing. While milling around backstage, I saw a very "button down" kid making fun of the drummer, acting like he was pouring his Cola on the drummer's extra long coif. It took about a 1/16 of a second for drummer Phil Lowe to spin around and pop him on the jaw. I was as surprised as the kid, who had it coming, and once the kid gathered his senses he quickly back peddled, saying that he was just joking. This wasn't a big deal, but it still is in my memories as clear as the music that they played that day.

DANIEL COSTON: *New venues for teens began popping up all across town, eager to cater to the new scene.*

RANDY HALL: I first saw the Paragons at Joe's A Go Go, which was a teen club on Wilkinson Boulevard. The Young Ages played there, too. The first real teen club was the Spyder Web, at the YMCA. There was the Straggle Inn, which was at Myers Park Methodist. The Tin Can, at Christ Episcopal Church, that was my church. There was another venue at Trinity Church. The Spyder Web was the place where you could really play. And they paid you!

JAKE BERGER: The Crested T., the Tin Can. The Straggle Inn. That was a big one. There was another one at the corner of Sharon Amity and Providence. And Joe's A Go Go, on Wilkinson Boulevard. And of course, The Web. These places sold fruit juices, Cokes, and snacks with a small cover charge usually of about 50 cents. These clubs offered not only a variety of different teen bands for the kids, but were an invaluable resource for the musicians who were kids themselves, giving them a venue to hone their skills and to network their groups. At these teen clubs, I saw loads of groups, most of which I don't remember and probably gave only fleeting attention to, but there also many that were really good. They kindled my imagination, and gave me rough blue prints for what I wanted to do then, and later also re-kindled my enthusiasm when I got "re-invigorated" with music, and life in general.

CHUCK WHITAKER: The Spyder Web was in the basement of the YMCA. It had a sign over the door that said, "No one over 17 years of age allowed," though that wasn't always true. In its heyday, it was the place for local bands, or bands from around the region, as well as meeting place for a lot of people.

DON TETREAULT: The Web was a good place to find out if someone was into the music. You might have seen them at school, but you would not have known. But then you'd see them there, and you'd be like, "Wait a minute, I know them!" Later on, when the Phantasmagoria opened, that helped to bring together a lot of people.

DAVE LONG: We weren't in a big city. We had to make our own stuff, and create our own thing.

JAKE BERGER: I saw it as we were like London, or San Francisco, but just really small. And we had to make it up as we went along. I used to buy 45s at Eckerd's, or at

Grant's, which was downtown.

DON TETREAULT: I moved here in about 1965. The older brother of a friend of mine had a set of drums, and I went to their house to see them. I had never drums set up before. I was like, "Wow!" When I was 17, my dad got a set of drums from somebody. It didn't take long for all the musicians in Charlotte to know each other. We weren't going to be in sports. This was our own fraternity.

I was struggling not knowing the links of the verses. Now, it seems so simple, but back then, we never knew, we just jammed so much. Verse, chorus, verse, chorus. Bridge, verse, chorus, out. And they would say that they wanted to solo, then back to the bridge. Twenty minutes later, "Okay, how do we get out of this?"

DANIEL COSTON: *Rob Thorne spent much of 1965 and 1966 with the Catalinas, though his fashion sense was already suggesting his next move.*

ROB THORNE: I used to wear an animal fur of some kind. Like a long coat or vest, or something. I'd wear anything bizarre, it didn't matter what it was. Now, I didn't do that when I first got with them. I played the part and dressed like they did. I was kind of a Yuppie kind of a guy during that period.

But then after that hump in the mid-Sixties, I just went downhill as far as that stuff. Dressing and hair, and my taste in music. I think that I was the youngest person in the band, I was at the bottom of the pecking order in the band at that time, I had been so compliant for five, six years. I did everything I was supposed to do. I looked like they did. It was all part of a unitized thing, and then all of a sudden I started getting weird!

DANIEL COSTON: *By the spring of 1965, Barry Stacks and the Grifs were throughout Charlotte, and preparing to cut their first single.*

BARRY STACKS: By this time, we were playing around a lot. We got new equipment. We were a complete mimic of the Beatles, when we started. We had the Vox equipment, that we had to order out of a company in New York to get it. We dressed in suits. A couple of days before we recorded "Catch A Ride," the Stones released "Satisfaction". And I heard that fuzz-tone, and I went to a music store, and I said, "What is that? Whatever it is, I want one." And they said, "We just got one in." It was this thing called the Fuzztone. On the way to the studio, sitting in the back of our van, I worked out that little guitar part in the beginning of that song. We rehearsed it a couple of times, and Manny Clark, who was a DJ with WGIV, produced the song for us and got the sound just right. Just where I wanted it, which was balls to the wall on it, when the song opened up. We actually did the music take in two takes, and then we added the vocals on top of it. And then we did ["In My Life"] for the other side. I used an Epiphone semi-hollow body. I told Arnie, "I want this as nasty as it can be, so when it comes on the radio, those first few notes, people will know who it is. There'll be no question."

We had booked the studio for four hours, eight o'clock till midnight. The guy that was running the board for Arthur Smith said we had to be packed up and out of there by midnight. I said, "What are you talking about?" He said, "We're booked all night, after midnight." We did what we had to do, but as we were packing up, this other band comes in to start setting up, and it was James Brown and the Famous Flames. And Manny knew James, he'd interviewed him many times. And James said, "Why don't you and your boys sit up in the control room while we record?" They recorded eight or ten songs, then they headed out on the Chitlin circuit. These guys weren't musicians like we were musicians. They were trained, they read music. I didn't do that. I had to pay someone to sit in on a rehearsal so they could write the lead sheets, so I could copyright the music. It was a whole different kind of music.

"Catch A Ride" originally came out on a label called 5D. The masters were later bought by a guy who had a distribution deal with MGM. He had a label called AMG Records, and that was Arnie Geller. Arnie went on to a pretty successful career as a producer. When we were playing around Charlotte, one of the first and foremost things for us was to get airplay. So to get airplay, you had to do favors. And one of the guys that we usually did favors for was a guy named John Fox, over at WIST. Whenever John had a live performance at a school where a band was playing, he'd invite us over. We'd come over and do three or four songs, and then we'd pack up and go do our regular gig for money, and we wouldn't charge him anything. We became good friends with John, and then John took a job at a station in Detroit. We had friends across the river in Canada, at CKLU. When he went north, he took our record with him, and he started playing it in the Detroit market.

We were unprepared for what happened. It exploded. We worked for a long time off of that record. We worked out at Myrtle Beach, Spartanburg, Columbia, Hickory. All the way down to Birmingham, Alabama. We got a good reputation, and sometimes when a British band would be touring, they'd bring us in as the opening act. That's what happened with the Coliseum with the Stones. We opened for the Dave Clark Five, the Hollies and Herman's Hermits. When I got to open for the Kinks, I just fell apart. To me, they were the raunchiest sound that I had ever heard. We used

collection of Robert Crawford

The Grifs, 1966.

to get a lot of criticism for how we looked, until we got on stage and blew the doors off the place.

DANIEL COSTON: *Among the shows that the Grifs played with the Rolling Stones was in Charlotte, when the Stones headlined a show at the Charlotte Coliseum in the summer of 1965.*

BARRY STACKS: It was us, the Trojans, and the Stones. Alan King, who was a local DJ, was brought in to host the show. He introduced us to the crowd as "Charlotte's own." For the Stones show, I was surprised on how few tickets they sold. It was a different beast, in Charlotte. The larger crowds weren't into the British invasion, yet.

SHORTY NEHRENBERG: The place was a little over half full. I thought that the show was great. That was my favorite period of the Stones. In retrospect, it probably didn't sound that great. There wasn't much of a PA, and any other sounds you heard was what you heard coming off the stage. But we didn't expect that much at that point, in terms of how a show like that might sound. When I saw the Beatles, you couldn't hear a thing! At least with the Stones, I could hear what songs they were playing.

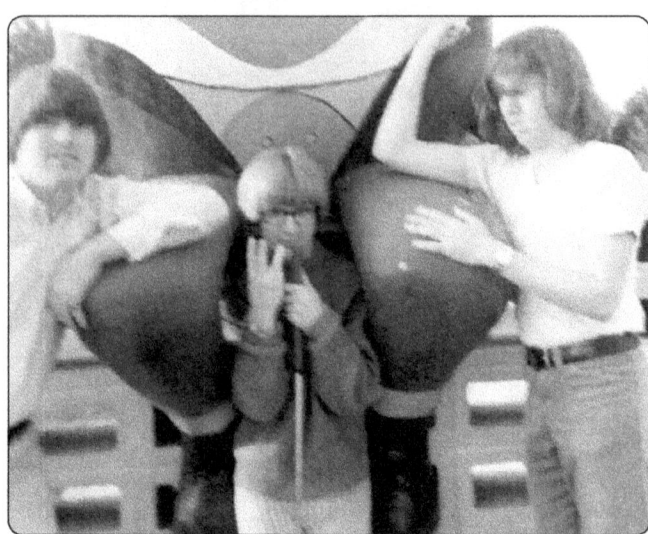

collection of Donny Fletcher

The Scotsmen, 1966.

BARRY STACKS: It took a long time for us to realize that if we were going to do anything, we had to get out of Charlotte. We had been making $150, $200 cash a week in Charlotte, which was good money back then. But when John Fox broke our record in Detroit, we got $2500 to come up there and open a show for a band called the Amboy Dukes. The Amboy Dukes, the Buckinghams and us at the place called the Mump, in Detroit. They had a rotating stage. When we were up in the Midwest, we could make a lot more money playing up there.

JAKE BERGER: The Grifs were like a mystery band to a lot of us in Charlotte. We heard about them, but never got to see them.

BARRY STACKS: "Catch A Ride" got a lot of airplay at WGIV, WIST, and Big WAYS. At one point, "Catch A Ride" was the number five record in town. Above us were the Beatles, the Kinks and James Brown. But where we really used to draw were the small towns. They'd put up posters of us, and people thought that we were English. They were surprised to learn that we were from Charlotte.

There a DJ in Hickory that opened up a series of teen nightclubs, all of which had Dragon in the name. Dragon's Lair, Dragon's Foot, Dragon's Breath. He had two of them in Charlotte, one on the west side, and one on the east side. We played a lot for him. He had one down in Monroe, one in Hickory, Myrtle Beach. There were a couple of places around town that held 200, 300 people, and we played those. And then we played at the high schools. They would have these dances, and they hired us to play them. We played at Myers Park, South Meck, and Garinger.

DANIEL COSTON: *Other groups, such as the Donny Fletcher and the Scotsmen, were making inroads to Charlotte.*

DONNY FLETCHER: My friend Scott and I were best friends. That's why we were called the Scotsmen. The first song I played on the drums was "Little Latin Lupe Lu."

We wanted to be in the club, but not quite in it. We wanted to be one foot outside the club. We were always looking for something different to play. Luckily, we were able to discover songs like "Little Black Egg". That searching is what led me to discovering English folk music, and Irish folk music a few years later. Just something different.

collection of David Floyd

The Gayelords, 1964.

We learned and stole a lot of songs from other bands. We tended to learn songs like "Gloria," which didn't have a lot of chord changes to them. We played Cramerton a lot. Then we played Gastonia a lot. There was a field house community center that we played there. We played at Belmont Senior High School, at a couple of dances. There was a place called the Purple Onion. That was a good place to play. Then we played Charlotte, which is where we wanted to play, because you're playing in front of people that we had seen play. If you could play at the Spyder Web and you went over well, then you had hit the big time. Then you'd run into these people on Sunday, and they'd be like, "Man, you were pretty good!" There was no scene in Gastonia, because

collection of Tom Pope

The Hodads, WAYS Battle of the Bands, 1966.

there was no alcohol, so you'd come to Charlotte to do everything.

We played a Battle of the Bands in Gastonia with the Gaylords, with David Floyd, who were really good, and a few other bands. I seem to recall that we finished second, but David Floyd says that we won. The Gaylords was the better band, and people voted for us because we looked cute. We were wearing Scottish plaid vests and white shirts, and black pants. It was a high school auditorium, and it was packed with people.

DAVID FLOYD: When I first played in a band, it was the Gaylords and we didn't know at the time that "gay" meant "gay". Well, first, it's spelled Gayelords, like the cartoon. Gayelord the dog, that's were we got our name. Not Gay Lords. And it was a kind of a Beatle band. And we wore the little uniforms with the vests, and there was a light-blue kind of look to everything, And we had Beatle boots that we dyed a glossy light blue. And we were playing up in Cramerton, where we had a little young, teenage girl-type fan club.

We weren't a big band at all. We were just a bunch of kids. We played a few Battle Of The Bands, and that's where I knew Don Tillman and Donny Fletcher from, because a lot of times we were competing against each other.

JAKE BERGER: I know that Donnie says that he always looked at you and the bands that you were in, and he probably saw you as a player as well, and said, "These guys are like the professional guys."

DAVID FLOYD: That was funny to hear him say that because we thought that they were the "professional guys"! They were doing the cool music though, and I don't remember what we were doing, like I said, we were doing all original music. I don't recall us ever doing any Beatle music.

That's all we knew. We didn't know anything about cover music or playing in a band that did that kind of music. It's funny how Donnie and [fellow Scotsmen member] Don Tillman recall us. We were just like the Scotsmen, they were a good band to be in. I heard about them all the time, and I thought they were the real deal.

DANIEL COSTON: *New bands began popping up in places throughout Charlotte. This included the Die Hards, and the Hodads.*

SHORTY NEHRENBERG: The Hodads lived down on Sharonview Road. The dad of a couple of the bandmembers did a lot of their management. I saw them at a lot of dances. They were really good, and sounded a lot like the Beach Boys.

collection of Jacob Berger
The Chapparals, 1966.

TOM POPE: When I was in 9th grade, I got a call one day from Guy Robbins. Guy was the singer for the Hodads. Their guitar player was quitting, and he asked me to join. And I said, "Yeah, sure." I'd heard of them, and knew that they did a lot of Beach Boys songs. I ended staying with them until I went to college.

We played a lot at the Cibo House Pizza. It was on South Boulevard. They had a lot of bands in there. The Web, the Straggle Inn. We did some bowling alley gigs. We all used to play out at Park Road Shopping Center. We'd play one Saturday, then maybe the Paragons would play the next Saturday. We played lots of private parties. People in Quail Hollow that had big houses. We used to play private parties for $16, or $20. It was lunch money.

We played gigs with the Grifs, and a band from Winston-Salem called the Satans. I don't know why they named themselves that. They weren't like that. They were paisley shirts, and were white kids playing Rock & Roll! We went as far as Charleston, SC, but we had to get our parents to drive us back then. Most of our gigs ended up being within 20, 30 miles.

When the Hodads started, they were doing almost all Beach Boys, and surfing instrumentals. However, Guy Robbins wrote some pretty decent songs, so we did a lot of originals around the time that I joined. Later on, the band got a keyboardist, and moved more into the British Invasion stuff. Guy and his brother Duffy, who was the drummer, had a great natural harmony, so we did a lot of harmony singing.

When I was at South Meck, there were a lot of bands that were going to school there. The Hodads, the Stowaways. There was the Chapparrals, who played a lot of British Invasion songs. And there was Shorty Nehrenberg and Dennis Edwards, who later formed the Modulation Blooze Band.

DANIEL COSTON: *By this time, the Stowaways were also starting to play throughout the region.*

TIM TATUM: One time, I was at a friend's house, and he pulled out this guitar case, pulled out the guitar and started to play. And I was just wanted more of that. The next Christmas, I got a guitar, and we just kept going. Tommy, our original lead guitarist, lived in the neighborhood, and we got together at his house and jammed around some. Eventually, we got some other guys in, and Ken Knight came in to play bass.

I really wanted to play guitar, but they wanted me to sing. The format back then was to have a lead singer. In fact, we had a guy who booked us wanted to call us "Tim Tatum and the Stowaways." We did up promo shots with "Tim Tatum and the Stowaways" printed on the photo. These guys went ballistic when they saw that.

KEN KNIGHT: We said, "What's this?" And we cut it off the photos.

TIM TATUM: I did have a lot of fun being the singer, though.

DANIEL COSTON: *The Stowaways were also one of the new Charlotte acts that made it into a recording studio.*

TIM TATUM: We went to Arthur Smith Studios once. We had won a WIST Battle Of The Bands at Park Center. Alan King was the MC. The winner got a recording session for Capitol Records, at Arthur Smith. It just meant that Capitol paid for the time. We played a Byrds song at the Battle Of The Bands. "It Won't Be Wrong." Tommy missed a couple of notes, and we kind of looked at each other like a deer in the headlights. We had camel jackets, with camel pants. We got all of our suits at Newberg's, on Trade.

KEN KNIGHT: We looked good. Our Beatle suits had been modified. We all had cherry red Gibson's. Guitars, and bass. For some reason, I stayed at Tim's house that night. The next day, his mother came in the room screaming, "You won the Battle Of The Bands!"

We really weren't ready for recording. This guy came down from New York, and said, "Show us what you've got." We were just doing covers at that point, so we just jammed out a song.

TIM TATUM: While we were there, James Brown came by to visit, and they couldn't come in the studio because Capitol had paid for the time. They told us that they couldn't come in because we were in the studio, and we were like, "Whoa!"

We traveled some. We played a lot of army bases. A couple of times, we'd skip school on Friday so that we'd get down to Florida, or Greenville, South Carolina for gigs on Friday and Saturday night. We were booked through a group called A&R Talent. They had a contract with the military. We played a lot of Air Force officers' clubs, and other places. We quit with them one night after a gig in Alabama. The promoter had given us the check, and the amount was twice as much as were told we were making. Usually, the check had been going to the agency. So I came back and talked to the agency, and they told me that it was for all these expenses. I went back to the band, and they said, "bulls--t." We had gigs at a couple of Air Force bases the next couple of weeks, and we just didn't show up for them. The agent called and swore that we'd never work in the Carolinas again, which we ignored.

After that, we were the house band at a place called the Rebel Lounge, which was down off North Tryon Street. We were not old enough to play the Rebel Lounge. One day, the owner came to us and said, "If anybody asks, you're 18." We would hang out in the parking lot, after the set.

BOBBY DONALDSON: I was playing places where I wasn't old enough to be in them. During breaks, I would have to go out to the parking lot, through a back door in the back of the stage.

STEVE STOECKEL: T.C. Atlantic was my first real band. In 1966, I teamed up with Tommy Smith, who lived a few doors away, and was a better guitar player. Back in those days, you had a Lead Guitar Player and a Rhythm Guitar Player. I was the latter. We eventually acquired a drummer, David Brakefield, and bass player (Karl Jarvi, and later Bobby Donaldson) and began murdering Beatles and Stones songs in the garage.

Then Denny Yager moved from Minnesota to next door, and brought with him a love for Paul Revere & the Raiders, and also a band name: T.C. Atlantic. It didn't mean anything, and I'd say it was a silly name if I hadn't been playing for a band called the Spongetones for the last 30-plus years. I have since found out that there was a semi-famous band with the same name, but this was pre-Internet. Who knew or cared?

So Denny became the lead singer, replete with a Mark Lindsay ponytail. We played at church rec halls, neighborhood parties, and high school functions. Low-profile gigs. We were a pop band. No heavy, bluesy, string-bending solos, but we were pretty good, heavy on the vocals. I left and was replaced by a much better guitarist, Marty Yandle, and the band lasted a bit longer. I took up bass guitar and, after a few years off, began playing professionally in 1970.

JAKE BERGER: T.C. Atlantic were a great band. I saw them at a Battle Of The Bands, and they played "Reach Out (I'll Be There)", and they nailed it.

STEVE STOECKEL: The Paragons and T.C. Atlantic opened up for the Catalinas at a club called The Box in 1966. Rob Thorne was with the Catalinas, so we had three future Spongetones onstage at the same time. We were embarrassed because the Paragons and T.C. Atlantic had both shopped at Mr. Hi Style before the gig, and bought cool shirts, of the same style! Theirs were blue and ours were gold, but they were the same. It was like girls wearing the same dresses to the prom.

JAKE BERGER: In the fall of 1966, school sessions began. I remained in the 7th grade, the result of me "pissing off from my responsibilities". Into the school year, I met another kid that I kind of known from other circles. We went to the same church, when I was snagged into going, that is. He was a quietly confident guy that was always polite and friendly and this was Doug James. Doug now is a respected classical guitarist and professor at Appalachian State University, in Boone, NC. Doug still displays the quiet confidence and congeniality that he showed when I first met and got to know him.

Doug had a Silvertone bass and a Silvertone amp, and I lost no time making plans with him and my old buddy, Ronnie Smith. Here was a chance to form a real group and not even have to travel across town to play a little music! In 1965, I had met a kid that was somewhat of an outcast because he had moved to Charlotte from the Midwest, and was not a "born to the manor" Myers Park silver spoon baby, or a "Banlon Baby", as we were starting to call them, because of the style of shirts that they wore. This was my buddy Gary Plavidal, and he was a real live drummer. He had a kit of Slingerland's, and his dad was fine with us framming out a big racket in their garage. Doug and Gary, along with my old running partner Ronnie Smith and I, set to it.

We learned about six or seven songs, and this is when I first started working with other people to make a concerted effort to make and perform music. This would be, other than a brief duo gig at the neighborhood church with my sister and an acoustic guitar, the first group I would actually play with in public before a live audience. We played at St. Martin's church youth hall, on 7th street in Charlotte. There were probably nine or ten people

The Young Ages, 1966.

there, and our set consisted of songs like "Gloria", "The House Of The Rising Sun", "Wipe Out", and probably "Louie Louie" was smirked out at some point. We even had a name for ourselves. We were The Ajents, and we would spend the next few months practicing in Gary's garage.

I can't remember if we ever did another show or not. Probably not, but I did print cards in shop class, where, since "hair" was becoming an issue, the shop teacher Mr. Baldwin would address me as "Ringo" and just about have a fit each time, because he thought he was so funny. On the other hand, by this time I was pretty good at ignoring adults or anybody else that tried to assert authority. I had been allowed to move to the house of my bed-ridden granny on Moravian Lane. This suited me to a "t", I had the whole upstairs of the house, that and my pal Doug James lived on the street behind us. The upshot of this arrangement was that I could come and go as I pleased, any time of night or day without the knowledge of my grandmother.

DANIEL COSTON: *In 1966, the Young Ages formed at North Mecklenburg High School. The phrase that they eventually take as their rallying cry was, "Brothers To The Bone."*

JOHNNY BARKLEY: The Young Ages came together from two different bands, the Bar-Talks, and December's Children. It was Mark and Dickie [Carrigan], or Mark and Ronnie talking together.

RONNIE PHILLIPS: We all knew each other through school. We had won a talent contest there, where we dressed up and wore Beatles wigs.

MARK MYERS: I really liked the singing of Eric Burdon, with the Animals. I really liked being the lead singer, although I could never dance to save my life. I would just stand in one place, and try to remember the lyrics.

DAVE LONG: I grew up near the Young Ages. They were my buddies. We used to hang out in Ronnie's basement, playing music. I was the token harmonica player. We had hormones and electric guitars. We had a lot of fun. No Vietnam, yet. We didn't have a care in the world.

DANIEL COSTON: *Billed as the first Hard Rock band in Charlotte, the band began to build a following in Charlotte. They also commandeered a bread truck as the band's mode of travel.*

DAVE LONG: It was an old square bread truck. Somebody painted it red, white and blue. These days they'd tell you that you couldn't take that out of the barnyard. Yeah, you could!

The Young Ages was the first band I photographed. One time, the Young Ages were playing the Purple Penguin, and we decided that we needed to step it up. I wore an orange and white striped turtleneck, and some kind of vest like Sonny Bono, with bellbottoms. Bob called it my "orange orangutan suit," I guess because of the orange color.

BOB ROBINSON: We were the first band to ever play at the Purple Penguin, and we helped open it up. We happened to walk in there when it was being built, and started chatting with the owners. Originally, they had planned but a small dance floor, and a go-go dancer. And we said, "That will never make it." We helped them put the stage together, and we played the first night, and we kicked butt. The place was packed.

DAVE LONG: The Purple Penquin was a big-ass fancy disco on the corner of Central & Pecan. It had lights, a stage, and a lighted dance floor. Places for go-go dancers. We only played there one, or two times. Johnny Barkley and I were doing kid stuff one night. Punching each other in the arm, giving each other wedgies, and we got into a wrestling match. Kid stuff. So we were wrestling, and a couple of alcohol cops threw us out. "Are you drunk?" "No, sir. We're not even old enough to drink." Unfortunately, that meant that we could not play there anymore.

MARK MYERS: Only a couple of us were old enough to be playing the Purple Penquin, at the time.

DANIEL COSTON: *The highpoint of the Charlotte music scene during 1966 might well have been the Big WAYS Battle of the Bands. Twenty-seven bands performed at the all-day event, featuring several of Charlotte's top bands, as well as others from across the Carolinas. Who won the contest is lost to the memories of many, but for those who or did not play, it was a place to be seen by all.*

MIKE RAPER: I remember that. We weren't playing, but we were there. We wore polka-dot shirts.

TOM POPE: The Battle Of The Bands was crazy. You'd pull up, and everybody had their gear in little piles. You had five minutes to set up and start playing, and then you'd only play a few songs, and then you had to get offstage. Everybody was in stations, ready to go. I couldn't tell you how it sounded, but it sure was fun.

DANIEL COSTON: *However, one Charlotte band did stick in the minds of many from that day. A new group called the Paragons, and a song they performed called "Abba".*

A Song Called Abba

JAKE BERGER: At that Battle Of The Bands, I remember a group from the west side, the Die Hards, who had their guitarist tape his hand up, and got the M.C. to blather on about how they were going to, "Play for you even though he has a broken finger!" There was also a band whom I remember nothing about, except that they did a spot-on version of "The House Of The Rising Sun", with the drummer either really fainting during the song, or faking it. It was all about image and show business, back then.

The single most striking thing at the Battle Of The Bands was a local bunch, all in their early teens called the Paragons. I can remember watching their performance and being awed by them from the opening chords, to the extra long hair and to the energy that they exuded. They opened their set with "My Little Red Book", a song that was an underground hit, played by Arthur Lee and Love. I can't recall now if there was another song in their set, but I remember like it was yesterday their last tune. It was an original tune, unusual in those days, with the odd title of "Abba," written and sung by guitarist and vocalist Jim Charles. "Abba" was an instant garage band classic. One thing I remember thinking, or maybe just having a feeling, or desire as I left the Coliseum that day, that I would soon be up there. In public, looking sharp, and playing with a band.

DANIEL COSTON: *In 1964, Jim Charles was an aspiring musician, and fourteen year-old kid living in Killeen, Texas. Jim's father was a career Army man, and their family had moved several times in the previous years. Jim and his older brother Bill had spent the past year taking in the new sounds from England and America, with Bill playing bass and singing in his own group, the Lily Whyte Lyres.*

JIM CHARLES: It was December 20, 1964. My brother had just come back from college. He had gone into college early, to up his ROTC grades.

BILL CHARLES: Although he was four years younger than me, Jim was the one that got me into music. He was a much better musician than I was. For Jim, it was pure music. For me, it was, "Hey, this is cool, and maybe I can get a girlfriend."

JIM CHARLES: There was a cartoon, on a typical narration of the news today. I want to say Warner Brothers, or something of that nature. And there were these vaudevillian schticks like, "Eh, what's up doc?" Only it wasn't Bugs Bunny. Stuff like that. And one of them was a Middle Eastern character who would sound like, "Abba dabba dabba dabba." So, I started using that word in place of "blah, blah blah." "Abba abba abba." Then it turned into, "abba".

BILL CHARLES: The song started in response to our father, and him always telling us to turn out the lights, turn out the water. We had a lamp in our room, a cheap plastic 1950s lamp, and we put a red light to be cool. "Ooh, red light district."

JIM CHARLES: That was the lamp that our dad was always wanting us to turn off, so that became the "Abba lamp."

BILL CHARLES: Later, the lyrics were adapted to be about a girl, but originally, it was, "He came up to me", and said, "Turn out your lights." Turn out your lovelight, he's trying to break up a relationship. Our parents would do that. If a girl called me up on the phone, my mother would go berzerk. "Girls do not call boys." Anytime Jim dated, or I dated, they were really scrutinizing. "Who is she?" They thought we were up to something. So dad really would turn out the lovelight! The metaphor for turning out the light, was also turning out the lovelight.

collection of Jim Charles

Jim Charles, Freedom Park, 1968.

JIM CHARLES: He'd pop in [our room] all the time and tell us to turn off the lights, and we'd click it back on just as soon as he'd leave the room. About eight or nine o'clock.

Man, its just electricity, and we didn't pay for it in our houses. But he'd act like we had to cut it off, because we're wasting electricity. "Hey, boys, turn that light off!" So, he heard me call him "Abba." So, he stopped and came back and says, "What did you say?"

And I remember that he punished me and told me to go and look that up and then think about what you said and write it down. That was sort of the way that he punished. An army belt just didn't work. I'd lock myself in the bathroom and count to a hundred, and then negotiate with him until he'd finally give up.

I really didn't know what to say, except that I liked playing. I had a cheap, plastic, imitation of a guitar. They sold them at Ward's. And I had a Gibson. An old F-holed Gibson. And [a friend] showed me the basic chords to, "House of the Rising Sun" which, aside from G, there it was. You could take any chord and move it anywhere, and maybe it would work! New Song! Bar chords! New Songs!

He came in there and basically said, "What have you thought about?" And I basically didn't realize what "Abba" meant. It means, "Father." And it is just not reverent to say it in terms such as that cartoon. It was not politically correct. So what Pop basically wanted me to do was to think about what I'd said, and apologize to him and say that I was sorry that I'd said that. But he said along with it, "You've got to cut your hair." At the time I was trying to do an "Elvis" and comb it out. Not like a Beatle type, but combed out. I guess that he was responsible for getting me that stuff from that drugstore that greased it out, which I thought was cool, and I caught hell for that!

But the thing was he did bring some points up, like, "stop your drinking", which I really didn't drink, and "stop your smoking." A cigarette was a really cool thing to have. I was stealing Mom's Salem's, and Dad's Camels.

BILL CHARLES: Later on, we were sitting around, "mooning and Juning." I was the one that wrote down on a piece of paper our ideas, and we would bounce ideas off each other. Jim had a guitar, and he would say, "Write this down." He was the creative force behind that song.

DANIEL COSTON: *Soon after, "Abba" was debuted in the Lily Whyte Lyres, which played around the Killeen area.*

JIM CHARLES: Bill said, "Let's take that lamp, and put it on stage, and click on that red light."

BILL CHARLES: At the start of the song, I would turn the lamp on, and at the end of the song, I would dramatically go over to the side of the stage, and turn the lamp off. That was our light show, in those days.

DANIEL COSTON: *In the late spring of 1965, Jim's father was reassigned to Vietnam, and his brother Bill went into the Army. Jim and his family then settled in Charlotte, NC, where Jim's parents had bought a home on Idlewild Circle in the 1950s.*

JIM CHARLES: My uncle used to rent that house out, and I came to visit Charlotte a couple of times when I was growing up.

DANIEL COSTON: *Soon after moving to Charlotte, Jim was walking to the Nature Museum at Freedom Park, when he heard a band playing in one corner of the park.*

JIM CHARLES: I heard this band performing "Tobacco Road." And it was the Abbadons. And I said, "Can I sing with you guys?" And they said, "Sure, we don't care to sing." And there I was.

DANIEL COSTON: *The roots of the Abbadons had begun the year before, when brothers Larry and Jimmy Duckworth had been kicked out of the school marching band for having long hair.*

JIM CHARLES: Larry and Jimmy Duckworth's daddy gave them a lecture that "they kicked you out of the band, but if you cut your hair, I'll get you guitar lessons at Howren's, up the block." Of course, Jimmy wasn't happy, and of course he only got like a half-inch cut off his hair, but he became one of the premier guitarists because of those lessons.

    Not too long after that, my mom took me to Charlottetown mall, and I was there in my crazy clothes. And there were some other guys there in crazy clothes, and it was Johnny and Bobby [Pace], and Danny [Huntley]. And that's how we [and the Paragons] met. And they said, "Do you have a guitar? Would you come over on Wednesday?"

DANNY HUNTLEY: I got involved in music when I went to the now defunct Tillman's Music, off Independence Boulevard, and looked at guitars, being that the Beatles and others were the rage, and I saw a Gretsch Guitar that I really wanted. It was a Chet Atkins Gretsch. My dad reluctantly but finally bought it for me and I started music lessons there, too. That was my start in music.

While at Cochrane Junior High (Middle School now) I met Johnny Pace and Danny Partis and we shared our common interest and brought together a band. We practiced at Danny Partis' home, and played at some functions, probably "sock hops" at Cochrane, mainly. When Danny Partis moved back to California, Johnny's little brother Bobby joined as a bass player.

JIM CHARLES: Originally, we were the Pagans, and Mrs. Pace had her thesaurus out on a Saturday, and we were having a vote [about the name]. She looked up Pagans, and down a little further was Paragons. So she actually came up with the name, out of the book, and then we voted on it. I kept thinking, "It kind of sounds like a parrot, but okay."

collection of Jacob Berger

Jake jamming with Johnny Pace, 1972.

DANIEL COSTON: *Jim ended up playing with both the Paragons, and the Abbadons, with both bands playing an impromptu Battle Of The Bands at the swimming pool of Sedgfield Junior High that summer.*

JIM CHARLES: I met Pat Walters there. Larry Duckworth knew him. He had his guitar there, and his army coat, even in the summer.

DANIEL COSTON: *By this time, both bands were also playing "Abba", with each band doing a different version.*

JIM CHARLES: The original first and fifth verse of the song, "She didn't know what to say", Johnny Pace sang that, and I would sing "I saw Abba late last night," when we would sing, and leave out the other verses.

It was completely different by that time. It was still the same melody, but just changing the words to that poppy kind of thing. [Johnny] said, "Get your haircut, girl" and that started a little argument. "No it's not 'girl,' okay! Don't try to change everything!" Like that was so important! Naturally it was, but just changing the words to that poppy kind of thing, "She looked at me and I could tell she'd be mine." I just didn't like that. I didn't want that in it. It just didn't fit with the other words. So there was a little battle. There was always a little battle of the bands within The Battle Of The Bands. That was just one of those moments in time.

Even in those early days, the Pace's had wonderful equipment. Bobby had already received that Hofner Beatle bass. And I was hard-pressed for my mom to get me the latest and greatest Vox guitar. So she did, of course. Johnny and I played at Belk, for a fashion show. I remember one request. "Do 'Moon River.'" The Pace's knew enough people [to get gigs]. They were a wonderful family, as was the Duckworth's. We played that Irwin Building, for a garden party, outside. We played the South 29 Bowling Lanes, and we did really well at the Alamo, which was a hotel that is no longer there.

DANIEL COSTON: *In early 1966, a huge Battle Of The Bands was held at the Charlotte Coliseum, with 27 local bands signed up to play. The Paragons had high hopes for the event, but other events would soon get in the way of Jim Charles, and the rest of the band.*

JIM CHARLES: My supposed girlfriend decided to like Johnny, and her sister told me that. So I got all big and huffy-puffy on the telephone. "I'm going to come and beat you up, Johnny!" That was not a mistake. I was a kid! And [Mr. Pace] said, "Don't you ever come back here again."

DANIEL COSTON: *Despite all of this, the Paragons placed eleventh at the Battle Of The Bands, with many in the crowd feeling that the band should have scored higher.*

JIM CHARLES: The winner was a band that was a little older than us. They did "House Of The Rising Sun," kind of rocking, and raunchy. And then they pushed their equipment over, like the Who. I'd never seen that! And after the show, I never went back. He should have let us little boys wrestle it out, because we would've made up, anyway. Kids are kids. Talk it out, if nothing else. And it was silly. Later, Johnny passed away, and I never got to talk to him again. And that's terrible.

DANIEL COSTON: *With Jim Charles out of the band, the Paragons did not have to look far for his replacement.*

JIM CHARLES: I remember Pat Walters was at the Battle Of The Bands, with his army coat, and his Maltese cross around his neck. He was playing with [Paragons organist] Tim Moore at that gig, because they mish-mashed the Paragons with the Barons, for the gig.

JAKE BERGER: I thought I looked so cool in my striped jeans and military jacket, not suspecting that "alternative fashion" had just taken a radical step forward. I was taken back for a second, until I recognized him as the guitarist I had seen with the Barons a few months before. Here was Pat with a huge amount of hair, that looked like a giant bird's nest turned upside down on his head, white corduroy pants and a large iron cross that had been cut out of a Chiquita banana box logo, in a public display of nose-thumbing.

PAT WALTERS: Tim Moore went to Garinger. I was still in Junior High, Eastway, and he said, "Hey, there's this guy named Johnny Pace." I kind of knew the Paragons, but he became more acquainted with The Paragons. While the Barons were still going, in the summer of '66, teenage bands could play at rec halls, the parks, like Revolution at the swimming pool. I don't know who put these things on. But you'd go there and there'd be three or four bands playing, so you'd meet kids from different places in Charlotte. So, I became acquainted with The Paragons. So, we thought, "That Johnny Pace really can sing well, why don't we see if he will be our lead singer? I believe he sang with the Barons on part of a gig, or something, just kind of went up and sang lead. But, he was a drummer. Plus, he was in a band with his brother, so, he wasn't about to break up the Paragons.

DANIEL COSTON: *Despite opening for Herman's Hermits at Memorial Stadium the previous year, as well as playing some other high-profile gigs, the Barons were on their last legs by the summer of 1966.*

PAT WALTERS: The Barons were kind of falling apart, and Tim joined the Paragons. And I started hanging out with them. And then there was some sort of falling out with Jim Charles. And they said, "Maybe we should talk to Pat Walters, and see if he'll play with us". So, I started going up to the Pace's house. They had a great place to practice. They had this little house. It was a pool house, a little house for playing pool, with their pool table in it. And they had their amplifiers, and their dad would lug them around in his Ford panel truck. And this seemed really cool and efficient, and they were really great guys.

ZAN MCLEOD: Leroy [Pace], he was a TV repairman. He kind of pulled them together, and got them a sound system, and a car, and he made sure they got to places on time. He helped them book the gigs. He was really a kind of "stage father" to them, I don't know if they could have pulled it all together without Leroy. He was great. I remember seeing them at the Park Road shopping center. They pulled up in a hearse. The doors would open and those guys would get out. And there would be all these girls trying to get their autographs. It was just like they were Rock stars!

DANNY HUNTLEY: We painted The Paragons on the windows. I had my driver's license before the others, so I was the appointed driver. It was quite a site going down the road.

RANDY HALL: The Paragons were a great band. Three-band harmonies, and they looked like they were British, but they lived right down the street! If they can do it, we can do it! Grow your hair out. They were way ahead of everybody.

PAT WALTERS: So I started playing with them. And then a few months later, this manager lady [Bobbie Cashman], who was probably all of about 24 years old, I think, came around and said, "Oh, I can make you guys stars," and "You should record a record." So we recorded a single.

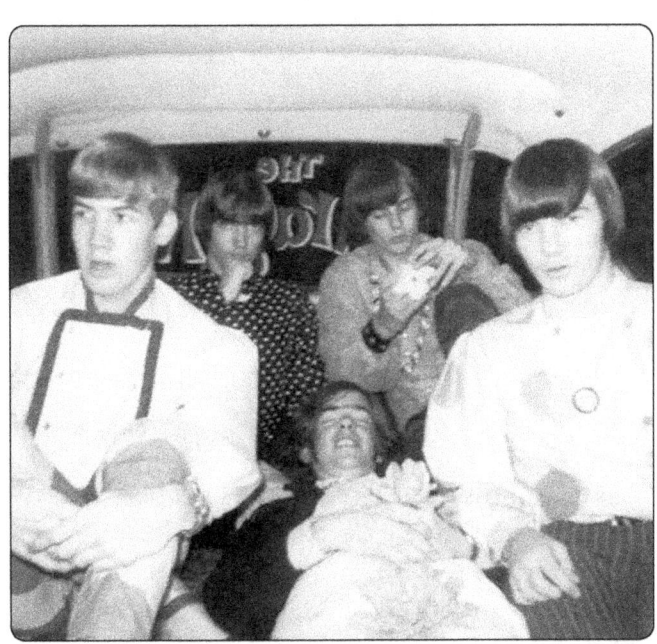

photo by Leroy Pace, collection of Pat Walters

The Paragons traveling in their hearse, 1967.

DANIEL COSTON: *Soon after, the Paragons put together a recording session at the Arthur Smith Studios. The Paragons brought two songs to record. The Yardbirds' "Mister You're A Better Man Than I," and "Abba."*

PAT WALTERS: It was probably an afternoon or evening session. Not a full day, maybe four to six hours for both songs. We were all excited about being there. There wasn't much overdubbing, they didn't have many that tracks to work with. I'm sure that the vocals were recorded apart from the rhythm track. I remember all of us around one mic for the backups. I remember it as being fun. We were big fans of the Yardbirds, who had recorded "Better Man Than I" on an album. It was probably suggested by

collection of Pat Walters

The Paragons performing on television, 1967.

me and Johnny Pace. I'm not sure how I came to use a 12-string on ["Abba']. I'm sure that I thought the guitar part screamed out for one. My friend Dave Long loaned me his for the session, and I bought one similar to his guitar shortly after that. The session was produced by Manny Clark, a black DJ at WGIV. He was brought in by the manager, Barbara "Bobbie" Cashman. We used the studio's amps. I recall brown face Fender amps. A Fender Concert, in particular. They sounded great! I still had a Maestro Fuzz Tone, at that time. It used to clam up in the Pace's little house when the weather was cold, before they turned on the gas heat.

DANIEL COSTON: *Tagging along for the session, Dave Long also became a part of the recording itself.*

DAVE LONG: We didn't go to school together, but we lived on the same side of town. I was buds with Pat, and the Pace's. I was a regular hanger-outer at the Pace's. One of the engineers or producers said that the recording needed a tambourine. I picked one up, shook it, and he said, "Yeah, that's it!" A 12-string and a tambourine goes together! Man, we were excited, pumped up. The guys nailed it! They knew their parts, such young pups with those high voices!

JIM CHARLES: It was meant to be, that Pat Walters played on "Abba." He put that kind of Middle Eastern chord on it that made it sound so cool.

DANIEL COSTON: *Pressed on the Bobbi label, named after Cashman, "Abba" became a huge local hit, and received airplay throughout the Southeast.*

Jake with Bobby Pace at The Web, 1969.

PAT WALTERS: They even played us on WGIV, and that was a soul station. I can remember being at school over at Eastway with my transistor radio with the wire running up my hand, when I should have been paying attention in school, I was listening to the radio. And they played it on jukeboxes all over the place.

GILL VANDERLIP: That song was the "I Wanna Hold Your Hand" of Charlotte, North Carolina.

DEBBY DOBBINS: Oh, we thought it was fabulous! We loved it and we played it and played it and played it and played it! We said, "We know these guys, they have a record!" And we'd go to hear other bands and other bands just weren't up to snuff compared to The Paragons! The Paragons just were better!

DANNY HUNTLEY: We sold it in schools, with me at Independence High in its first year of existence, as a sophomore, and Johnny and others at Garinger High. The reception was very good and we sold most of the lot. Some of the bullies I recall remarked such things as, why would we pay you two dollars for a local record when we can get the Buckinghams and their hit song for the same price? But, we soon had a following as I arranged for the Paragons to play at a dance at Independence. A success!

STEVE STOECKEL: I remember Tim Moore prowling the hall at Garinger, with a bunch of the "Abba" 45's in his hand, asking people if they wanted to buy a copy.

PAT WALTERS: [On the "Abba" 45] credits it says, Danny, and Johnny. When the record came out, I was surprised to see that Jim Charles' name wasn't on the label.

DEBBY DOBBINS: I didn't know who [Jim Charles] was. At that point in time we were all too young and stupid to look and see who wrote anything.

"Abba" registration form in Bobbie Cashman's handwriting, listing Jim Charles as co-author, 1967.
collection of Jim Charles

JIM CHARLES: When I saw them on "Kilgo's Canteen" [TV show], I called the Huntley's house, and Bobbie just happened to be there. And she said, "Well, there's not a damn thing that you can do, it's been recorded!" But what upset me, I went and bought the record up at Park Road. And I didn't see my name on the label. It said, "D. Huntley and J. Pace." And I broke the record up into many pieces.

DANIEL COSTON: *Cashman would later send Charles a BMI registration form for "Abba," which listed Charles as co-writer, along with Bobby Pace, and Danny Huntley as arranger.*

JIM CHARLES: I'm sure that [Cashman] just took the people there, and went with it. Johnny sang the words, but he didn't write the words. Danny was the guitar chord guy, he may have written down the notes, and they said, "That looks like an arrangement to me." I don't think they were mean, horrible people. It was just not discussed.

DANIEL COSTON: *So who wrote "Abba"? We have established that Jim and Bill Charles created the original version of the song, and performed the song in Texas, and in Charlotte with both the Paragons, and the Abbadons. Credit should also be given to Johnny Pace for his restructuring of the lyrics, and to Danny Huntley, Pat Walters and the rest* *of the band for their contributions to the version that was enshrined in vinyl. Special note should also be made for Manny Clark, who in a year produced two of the most amazing songs to ever come out of Charlotte, "Abba" and "Catch A Ride".*

After the Paragons, Jim Charles rejoined the Abbadons, who by this time had built up their own safe haven of music.

LARRY DUCKWORTH: I can easily encapsulate the phrase, "The Little Rascals of Rock", by saying that it was a bunch of kids who trying to figure out, with whatever resources they had, how to put together a rock band! I remember it wasn't long before my brother could go to Lowe's hardware and get a guitar. Then I made a big deal with my parents, and they bought me a few drums.

And then later on, with things like light-shows, we went out and bought a bunch of floodlights and put colors on them, nailed them into the wooden crates. It was like, "What are we gonna do next?" And we'd get floods and we'll have switches, and we'll get a lampshade, spray paint it, drill holes, put the switches in there and hook the lights up to that. So we had a light show! It was basically two wooden crates, eight floodlights and a lampshade and some switches!

My parents had a wonderful house that had two complete basements! And the upper basement was just a giant clear area where you could set up a band! And so that was the neighborhood rehearsal spot! Plus, it was removed enough from the rest of the house that my parents could live their lives in some degree of peace. Though, not much! Also, my parents were just very open to people. You know, they weren't all about being strict about this and that. I mean, we had our definite rules, but my parents were very warm and inviting. Their philosophy was that they would rather all the other kids came to "be with our kids at our house, because then we know where they are and what they are doing".

JAKE BERGER: During the winter of 1966, I had met and made friends with a kid, Randy Turner who played drums with some kids from Sedgfield Junior High. I ended up playing with them until the spring of 1967, and through Randy met the young guitarist from the Abbadons, Jimmy Duckworth. Jim lived a half mile from me and it was there that the Abbadons rehearsed. The Abbadons consisted of Jimmy on guitar, brother Larry Duckworth on drums, a nice sort of bohemian fellow, Cliff Davis on guitar, Gaines Brown on bass, and by this time, ex-Paragon Jim Charles, also on guitar and vocals. Jim was a fiery singer in the screaming soul manner, and a really nice guy. He was one of those guys that didn't "talk down" to you, if you happened to be a few years younger.

I saw them play a few times. One gig that sticks to the memory is a show they did at Rosemary and Bill Heptigue's house one weekend, while their parents were away. This was a common occurrence during that time period. Parents gone, house party! I remember them doing "Shake A Tail Feather", a song that was fairly new at the time.

Somehow, I got invited to a house party at the Duckworth's one Friday night. I snagged a bottle of whiskey from God only knows where, and brought it out at the party. Larry, who was older and certainly wiser, calmly asked to see it and promptly threw it out. I knew that he was a black belt, and for once kept my mouth shut, although he didn't act in a manner worthy of a bully, nor make a big deal out of it by doing it in front of everybody. So in retrospect I realized that he was, while keeping a lid on things at his parents, wasn't being a bully. So I had no complaints, and I probably didn't care as at that time, I was, as kids will do, just trying to "be cool" and had not yet become a drinker.

DANIEL COSTON: *Jim Charles continued playing with the Abbadons until early 1967, although he stopped playing "Abba" soon after the Paragons released their version of the song.*

JIM CHARLES: After I saw [the Paragons] do it, I didn't want to do it anymore. Also, they had a different edge to their music and it was just too pop. I love singing that song now, but that was how I felt at the time.

CHAPTER FIVE
Instruments and Gear

DANIEL COSTON: *By 1965, an aspiring musician in Charlotte could find more places to get the newest records, and the new trends in clothes. No discussion of musical instruments in Charlotte is complete without the legendary Melvin Cohen and Reliable Music, which became a staple of the local music scene for nearly four decades.*

JAKE BERGER: Melvin Cohen probably helped the music community here along more than anybody. He talked his dad into allowing him to run a small musical equipment shop in the back room of his dad's pawn shop, Reliable Pawn & Loan, on Trade Street. Reliable is where I got my first guitar, a Silvertone acoustic. It was a sort of reward for achieving passable levels when I was in the 6th grade. Melvin sold it to my dad, and I'm sure that whatever haggling was done, my dad came out on the short end of the stick. Melvin knew his business and of course had his father there to oversee and show him the ropes. I also got my second axe there. It was a Kay electric, and again my dad acquired it for me.

photo by Pat Walters

Melvin Cohen, late 1960s.

Melvin opened Reliable Music in the back of his dad's shop the day he graduated from high school. Melvin would let me and lots of other kids hang out in the shop and play and learn on the new gear that adorned the walls. He carried a nice line of equipment and was the only Rickenbacker dealership around here that I knew of. In the late Sixties, he carried the big Ampeg amplifiers, and I would see The G.B.U. play that particular gear. Melvin would loan stuff out to the Paragons, and the Young Ages. He did this out of friendship for them. When bands became a regular occurrence at Freedom Park, he supplied the PA systems, and helped organize the shows. He was responsible for importing regional acts for these shows, acts that would be outside of the mainstream of the day.

After escaping my infamous lost decade and becoming more involved with the local music scene that I had been in and then out of again for almost twenty years, I started to conduct more and more business with Reliable Music. By this time, Reliable was a huge boutique music store, and one of the first of its kind. Later on, I started to get to know Melvin on an adult basis, running into him at Sam's, or somewhere else. He would stop whatever it was that we were doing, and we would chat for some lengths of time, oblivious to the people meandering around us. In the process I found him to be a gracious and witty guy. Just a good bloke, as they say.

Reliable Music closed its doors in 2001, knuckling under to the large corporate music chain stores. Melvin may not have been a musician, or as Steve Stoeckel puts it, "Melvin never played an instrument. He played the cash register, and yet Melvin was more responsible for the music here than anybody". Sadly, Melvin succumbed to cancer and passed from this life in 2004. Rest In Peace, Melvin.

ZAN MCLEOD: Melvin started alternate music. He got that thing going at Festival in the Park, and then he got concerts in the summer and fall. He would just throw some stuff out there like Good, Bad And The Ugly, and bands like that, all the local guys. Melvin was the center of the music scene. I mean, Melvin was it. I got my first electric guitar from him. Everybody did.

I used to just go downtown on Saturdays, just to have something to do. I'd catch a bus and go downtown, I was a kid. And I'd go to Tanner's. Get a hot dog. Walk around, go to some of those clothes stores and look around, maybe buy something. Maybe buy a record. On Saturdays, there was nothing out here, you had to go into Charlotte to see anything.

Park Road Shopping Center was here but there was only like a shoe store and Eckerd's, a grocery store, but nothing much was here. And so, if you wanted to buy a record, you really had to go downtown to buy a record. I can't remember the name of that place. It was near Melvin's place. So we'd go downtown and we'd see guitars in the Pawnshop window, and we started going in there. And pretty soon he opened up another room in the back.

And so it was just an extension of the pawnshop, but it had guitars hanging up. And so that's how it kind of got going. They had drums, and whatever instruments. Pawnshops had everything. His dad, Joe was a great guy, and Joe sold watches, jewelry and gold, and all that stuff. He always had that little thing on his eye looking at diamonds.

I knew I wanted a Rickenbacker guitar and I knew that he sold them. And I could have a John Lennon-ish guitar. That was my first one. I wish I still had that. I traded it, a couple of years after that for a Gibson. I wish I still had that! It was a good SG!

DAVID FLOYD: Melvin's daddy wanted to know what he wanted for his graduation, and Melvin said that he'd like to open up a music store. And his dad didn't want to get a new place going, so he said that he could put it in the back of his store. And he gave him a line of credit and he bought guitars and stuff like that and that's how that store got started. It was way later before enough money came in to make it a real business venture.

PAT WALTERS: Melvin was really reaching out to kids like us, and other Rock bands. He liked the music, and he'd loan us stuff! Or he'd get something new, a new line, whereas the other music stores were pretty much evolved from "piano stores". A few of them, like Tillman's Music, or Neil Griffin had a store before that, that would have some Fender and Gibson guitars, but Melvin was more inclined towards our age group and our people who liked the kind of music we liked. So, he started hanging out with guys like the Young Ages, and I was hanging around with them, too. That's how Melvin and I became friends.

JAKE BERGER: I know that he did a lot. I heard that he'd lend out equipment. Hopefully you would buy it, but more often than not, it would just be "appropriated"!

PAT WALTERS: But, eventually his dad would go, "Uh, Melvin, where is this P.A. system?"

DAVID FLOYD: I know that Eric Clapton was a good friend of the store. And then later on, Steve Morse and the Dixie Dregs were good friends of the store. Years later, all of the Heavy Metal bands came in. And there were lot of clinics held there, so famous guitarists and famous drummers would come in for those.

DAVE LONG: Melvin from Reliable used to have a little tent out at Festival In The Park, and a little PA. That was a great place to see people play. That was the first time that I saw Jon Mullis play.

DAVID FLOYD: It was pretty important! Reliable was the only place I knew where the creative musicians were coming. All of the hippies coming in there like Zan McLeod. Everybody. You know, some of the bands like the Catalinas were already out playing before Melvin had a store, so they didn't go to him to get their stuff, they probably got it from McFayden.

JAKE BERGER: Before McFayden was there, I bet they got it from Tillman's.

DAVID FLOYD: Tillman's! Tillman's had stores in four or five cities!

JAKE BERGER: And they had a big one on Independence.

DAVID FLOYD: And that's where McFayden's wound up being later.

SHORTY NEHRENBERG: Back then, you would go to the store to buy strings, and so I'd buy a set of banjo strings and a set of guitar strings, and throw half of the guitar strings away, and use three of the banjo strings just to make a set of light strings, because they didn't sell them. And then we'd take like the old reel-to-reel tape recorders, turn everything up with the volume on High, plug your guitar into it like it's coming out backwards and send the signal into the amp so it makes it "fuzzy". Yeah we did all that stuff, until it caught on fire one night.

PAT WALTERS: I had a Fuzz Tone when I was still in the Barons. And they weren't very common, but when "Satisfaction" came out, that was like, "Okay! That's what he was using! A Maestro Fuzz." And I found one at Frank's Pawn Shop, down from the original Reliable, and they couldn't get it to work. Somebody had hocked it. And so I was able to get it cheap. Ten dollars, or something like that. And the reason it didn't work was because, instead of two jacks, it had a cord coming out, and the store thought that cord was supposed to go into the amp, but it was the input! I had to pay for my amplifier, my Fender amp. My sister signed for it, and I paid for it. It took about two years. Fifteen dollars a month!

JAKE BERGER: Did you get a new BandMaster?

PAT WALTERS: I did! It was great!

JAKE BERGER: I saw the Paragons playing at The Web one time, and Pat was doing the feedback. That must have been in early 1967, maybe. Pat had his Bandmaster up on the chair! And the tape recorder, he played it through the tape recorder to get that tube scream. It was like a pre-amp.

PAT WALTERS: There weren't all the pedals and stuff that you can get now. You had to really come up with the sound yourself.

JAKE BERGER: I remember you having that Esquire, and Gaines Brown had painted it all psychedelic, and I was like, "Yeah! Yeah! I wanna do that!"

DANIEL COSTON: *What kind of tape recorder was it?*

PAT WALTERS: It was like an Admiral, battery-powered type of deal with a three inch reels or maybe even smaller than that. So you actually had to put it in record mode, and I mean it sounded so "Hendrixy", it was like early Cream.

SHORTY NEHRENBERG: With folk music, you had to try to tune your guitar to every song, and every song on every record was in a different key, because that's how the taped slipped. It took you forever to tune up. We'd spend like four hours tuning and three minutes playing. It was just terrible. And then we finally got that strobe tuner and it was like, Holy Cow! I got to where I could use it pretty good, because it was like, "What a revolution!"

JAKE BERGER: A lot of the department stores used to sell 45s, and a handful of LP's. The record store that I went to was New York City Records, uptown. They had everything. And then you could go to Newburg's and get some clothes that nobody else had. I also remember Ernie's Records. Before he had the shop at Cotswold, he had a room in the back of Ernie's Hi-Fi and Camera, at Park Road Shopping Center. I used to go down there and I was just a little kid, I was like 12 years old. That guy was always good about saying, "Do you wanna hear that?" and he'd play stuff for us.

There was another store, Sustar's Music. I don't know about all the other kids, but I would skip school and eventually I just quit, and I would go downtown and play this guitar, and he was really good about that. He got killed by a robber. I was sorry to hear that. I mean, he was so supportive, and I know he hoped that eventually we would buy something and I did, but he was just so supportive.

DANIEL COSTON: *These days, if one wants to tell what year a photograph of the band was taken, all one has to do is look at the clothes. There is often a clear line between the show and beach bands before the British Invasion, and what came after it. In Charlotte, there was one store that carried all of the newest clothes. Some called it Newburg's, others called it Mr. Hi Style. It all was in fact one store, with the full name of Newberg's Mr. Hi Style.*

ROB THORNE: While most of the bands were buying their stuff at Mr. High Style downtown, the James Brown kind of outfits. The Catalinas were shopping at Tate Brown, and Mellons, and the Gentry House, so it was more collegiate looking for the most part when we dressed up to play it was really snappy looking, really great looking, after six tuxes and then coordinated Florsheim shoes, of course. We wore a lot of Weejuns back then.

JAKE BERGER: If you were looking for clothes, there was one place to go. Newberg's, on Trade Street. It was the only store in the state, and everybody would come in to get gear. There was later a couple of stores like that in Chapel Hill. It was Jewish-owned, black run store, and their deal was cutting edge. They carried records from New York that most chain stores didn't carry. It was the first place to find corduroy pants, with the big wide whale, polka-dot shirts. You could get flares, and later bellbottoms. You could get shirts with the white collar and cuffs. Big wide flower ties. And next door was a shoe store that carried Beatle boots.

DENNIS EDWARDS: Newberg's! We used to go to Newberg's! You had to!

PAT WALTERS: We'd wear the shirts with the white collars and the flowery shirts, and bellbottoms were just becoming available, and there we'd go to Newberg's Mr. Hi Style!

JAKE BERGER: They were the only ones that had it! They were the first to have flairs.

PAT WALTERS: Corduroy pants. Beatle boots. You could get some good ones for maybe ten bucks.

PAT WALTERS: Down at John Hardee Shoes, and Lebo's had some, as well.

JAKE BERGER: Hardee's was the first one to have the good Indian boots.

PAT WALTERS: They got into all the knee-high, suede moccasins and all kind of stuff like that.

JAKE BERGER: I had a tie that was really wide, and was flowered, and then I had a belt that was flowered that matched it, and a shirt with the white collar and cuffs. I wore that to school one day and caught all kinds of hell from the principal!

PAT WALTERS: I liked all the military-looking kinds of jackets that you could get!

JAKE BERGER: Yeah! With the high collars!

PAT WALTERS: And for not much money. Any of the stuff that I had, I had to buy myself. I come from a family of six children, so the little bit of money that I'd make playing at gigs, and I helped my dad out a little bit at the TV and Appliance store.

Memorable Shows

BOBBY DONALDSON: I loved the way that everything sounded in a live setting. Even if you were standing outside the concert hall, you could hear the slapback of the snare drum, and the way the other instruments sounded. And I remember thinking that it just sounded so good.

James Brown was unbelievable. He'd have three drummers on stage, and each one could kick your ass. And they had hardly any P.A. at his show. One big speaker on the left side, and one big speaker on the right. That was it. And they still totally kicked my ass!

I backed up folks like Arthur Conley. Backing up somebody was always difficult, but you did it. The singers would always come in late, and they'd walk in with a 45, and no one had a record player for us to learn the song. "We've got 30 minutes before we hit the stage. Can we do it?" But we always did it.

JAKE BERGER: I think it was at The Web, but George Ahramoonie was playing in some band, and he didn't have an organ. He had a vacuum cleaner with a hose, into the opposite end where it blows out, and had it rigged into an accordion, laid out on a table.

BOBBY DONALDSON: That would be George! He would make it work somehow. And the accordion is how he got to the keyboards.

DANIEL COSTON: *What do you remember about that Festival in the Park gig with the Greystones?*

BOBBY DONALDSON: I just remember being on that stage. We didn't care whether people liked what we were doing, we just did it! And it was probably over the top! I just remember Robert would be down on his knees and I'd be behind him with my guitar behind my back, and we'd work it out. I really don't remember seeing anybody else doing it, I just remember us doing it. I'm not saying we started it, but I honestly don't remember ever seeing anybody else doing it, it was just something that we would just do! That's all I know. I never saw anyone playing with his teeth, that's for sure! Of course, I found out years later that Jimi Hendrix didn't play with his teeth, he played with his tongue. I never knew that. I was the one with blood all over my guitar!

JAKE BERGER: Bobby Donaldson transferred to my school, Alexander Graham Junior High, and for the first two or three months was a sight, with his very long for the times hair parted in the middle, in order to affect the look of Dave Davies, of the Kinks. This didn't last that long and within a few months, Bobby had blended in with the kids in his class (he was ahead of me, grade-wise). Within six months, the school had a talent show, a common practice then and now for schoolsters. What I saw there blew me away, because without anybody knowing it, he had put together a combo with some other kids, notably with two singers who were black kids. At this point, I should say that almost until that year most of us had not been in a racially integrated classroom, and though integration had been the law for a few years, it was just starting to be put into practice. The world was changing for the better, but the growing pains had to be endured and were necessary for the change that was just starting to get into high gear, to happen.

Seeing the format, with Bobby "D" on guitar, Sammy Schifman on drums, Henry Lassiter on bass, Charles Vaden on trombone, and David Payne on trumpet, became the orchestra, and the two young "soul men" on vocals were a kid named "Willie Paul", and a classmate of mine, Johnny Benton. Soul Inc., as they called themselves, took the stage, opening with Junior Walker's "Hot-Cha", and for the second and final number, "Stand By Me", by Ben E. King. The professional sound and the performance itself was many steps beyond what I was seeing at pool parties and such, and was a great lesson on how it was supposed to be done.

SHORTY NEHRENBERG: We used to hitch-hike to shows out of town. A lot of the bigger bands weren't coming to Charlotte yet, at that point. This is when you could hitch-hike, and not worry about getting killed.

We hitch-hiked to Washington to see the Lovin' Spoonful. It was at the DAR Constitution Hall, and we got there hours early. We were there, just killing time, when we saw these guys trying to find an open door to go inside. It was John Sebastian and the Lovin' Spoonful. We talked to them, and they let us come in and watch soundcheck. After soundcheck, Dennis and I hid in the bathroom, and when the place was full, we walked back out and found ourselves a seat.

BOB ROBINSON: The Abbadons entered a Battle Of The Bands in Statesville, NC. This was during the time when psychedelic music was not in the mainstream, in the area. We were competing against all of the Soul, and R&B bands. We came on stage sporting long hair, Beatle boots and paisley shirts, contrasting with the tuxedos and banlon shirts worn by the other bands. Our song list consisted of "Purple Haze", "Tobacco

Road", and "Crystal Ship". After playing "Purple Haze", someone yelled, "That guitar sounds all fuzzy. It must be broken." Then we broke into "Tobacco Road", where in the middle break of the song we turned on the strobe lights, and Jim Charles would feign convulsions and collapse on the floor. Joe Duckworth, Larry's cousin, appeared with an old woven body basket to load up Jim's body and drag him off stage to then re-appear to finish the song. A few people booed us. Needless to say, we weren't very welcomed.

DON TETREAULT: I saw Jimi Hendrix open for the Monkees at the Charlotte Coliseum. The kids all booed him, and he walked offstage.

SHORTY NEHRENBERG: We snuck into the Monkees show to see Jimi Hendrix. As we walked up to the stage, Jimi put his guitar down, and walked off. That was all we saw! He left the Monkees tour after that night. We did stick around to see a song or two of the Monkees.

BARRY STACKS: The Stones, and the Kinks gigs were the best. [Mick] Jagger was a real asshole, but Ray and Dave were real down-home, and folksy guys. It was a pleasure. There was a couple of gigs in South Carolina with the Hollies and Herman's Hermits. They were a couple of hard-working bands. We sat around the hotel and talked to them for quite a while. Peter Noone was full of himself, but the guys in the band were normal Joe's. We did a series of show in Michigan at a place called Sherwood Forest. They had a bandshell, and we played with the Amboy Dukes, and the Buckinghams. The Kinks were not what I expected. They were not full of themselves. I knew after talking to Ray for ten minutes that this guy was operating some place else. He had a talent that if I could brush up against it, maybe I could get a little bit of it.

DONNY FLETCHER: My favorite gig used to be playing at a children's orphanage hospital. We would play there for the kids sometimes on Saturdays. We would help push the kids in wheelchairs, we'd play for them, and then we'd take them back. I loved it because my mom would say, "Oh, you boys were so nice to do that."

DEBBY DOBBINS: I can remember getting into the Cellar when I was thirteen on a fake I.D. to see the Guess Who. That was 1967. The drummer didn't show up, and the lead singer, Burton Cummings, had to play drums and sing.

SHORTY NEHRENBERG: Right after we moved to Charlotte, I went back to my friends in Memphis, and we rode the bus from Memphis to Atlanta and saw the Beatles. That

The Ravens, Harding High School prom, 1966.

was in 1965. That was really something. And my buddy, Danny, had the exact look, haircut and accent of John Lennon, he just looked just like him. It was during Lennon's kind of pudgy period, and this guy looked just like exactly like him.

So after the show we got down there, and he started sticking his head out the window at our hotel. We were on the third floor of a hotel down on Peachtree, and a crowd started gathering. Well, we were just kids, so we kept playing it up. It was also the first time I'd ever seen a bottle of liquor in my life, I was like 14, maybe 15, and before we knew it the entire floor that we were on was full of people and they were convinced that we were the Beatles in this hotel room. And so I went out to get something, and I couldn't get back to my room! I had to fight my way through the crowd. And I finally get back in the room and say, "What is going on?" And my buddies said, "They think we're the Beatles!" Then of course the manager of the hotel came and said, "If y'all don't come out here and tell these people that you are not the Beatles, I'm throwing you out right now." So we went out there and of course told them, but two of them still spent the night out in our hallway. They weren't quite sure.

I also remember that after we were walking away from the stadium after the show, and this car with a few guys was driving past concertgoers with a "I Hate The Beatles" sticker on the back of their car, and the girls were taking off their heels to punch a hole in the car as it went by.

CHUCK WHITAKER: Janis Joplin at the Park Center. She was amazing, and her nipples were poking through her outfit.

BOBBY DONALDSON: The Ravens opened up for the Four Tops and the Temptations once at the Park Center. We shared the dressing room with these guys. Of course I was just a kid! Just a young 'un! And I never will forget this one guy. It was "set up day" and it was at the Park Center, and he was the bass player, and the Motown guys brought down this rhythm section, and I think they hired some horn players who actually lived around here.

And this one guy, the bass player, he just kind of took me under his wing and talked to me all day, because the "scrub band", that's what we called the bands who started the show. The scrub band was us, and we didn't get to set up till the last minute, because we were first to go on. So this guy, I'd talked to him all day. He was a really nice guy. Not too many years ago I saw a documentary entitled, "Standing in the Shadows of Motown", and James Jamerson was that guy all those years ago who was talking to me all day long! And he is like the bass player for all of that stuff! The way that he played bass is a big part of that Motown sound!

DANIEL COSTON: *Did you guys struggle any with being white kids playing with black musicians? Did you get any stick from people? You were in the South when you were doing those shows.*

ROB THORNE: Not really. Because the audiences didn't care. Those kids didn't give a rat's ass about racism at that time. Most of them. And it didn't matter. The great thing about the Park Center is that if there were three or four bands on the show that night, there may have been three or four drum sets side by side up there. And each drummer would come up and use his set. And then sometime during the night, all three or four of us drummers would all be up there at the same time just wearing it out! And the crowd just loved seeing that stuff! They loved seeing a black guy and a couple of white guys up there on stage together.

We noticed, when we were traveling in the Deep South, during the Civil Rights Movement period, that we had trouble. Especially when we were traveling on a bus, and that would have been around '66 or '67, I can't remember, if we pulled into truck stops and stuff like that to get service or to get food, a lot of times we were told to leave because they thought that we were Freedom Riders. Because we didn't look like a band, necessarily, we looked like a bunch of college kids. Although maybe one or two of us looked like musicians. But most of us didn't. We dressed nicely and stuff like that. The mood was different only in the deeper south, along the bottom of the country. Where all the shit ran downhill and stopped. But in the Carolinas people in audiences were tolerant, very tolerant. Bands mixed nicely. We had a lot of black friends. There were a lot of black bands that we remained friends with for years, and we had a good time with them.

In the Carolinas, I don't think it mattered because people were so crazy about the bands that were making that music, and playing it on the radio. Now could be that in the Fifties it could have been a little different because the black artists, like Little Richard, who had some great hits with "Tutti Fruiti" and all that stuff, they could play to audiences. But they didn't play to white audiences the way the black bands did in the Sixties. That's why Pat Boone would do. His record label would get him to do "Tutti Fruiti", so the white guys did the black guys' music and had runaway hits with it. And could go out and do it in any venue that they wanted to. But the black record labels took a different approach to the whites'. As did the radio stations. And usually the commercial stations didn't play the black artists' renditions of those songs. They played the white artists' renditions of them during that period, the late Fifties.

Now there still existed, at that time, in Charlotte, at Park Center, when we would go see James Brown, all the whites sat upstairs in the balcony and all the blacks were downstairs on the floor with James. And the whites never went downstairs. You just never mixed. Because the energy down there was so highly charged and volatile because of James Brown and the excitement that was coming off of that stage, and of course they're all down there dancing and drinking and having a big time, and it was an amazing thing to see for a bunch of white guys. And almost band I knew in Charlotte, a white band, if we played that night, we'd go over to Park Center when we got through, sit in the balcony and watch James do his thing. But I never saw white people on the floor down there. You'd get hurt. Or at least that was the school of thought at that time. So, whites never mixed with blacks in that environment.

But now, there could be a multi-show. But rarely did blacks come to those shows and mix on the floor with white kids. That didn't happen, either. I think that maybe they stayed up in the balcony or maybe they just didn't even come at all to see the mixed shows, white and black bands. There might have been an exception with the Dick Clark Shower of Stars that used to come to the Coliseum.

They would have ten or twelve acts, like Lou Christie and maybe Billy Stewart or whoever was popular at the time. Fabian, people like that. They did all those kind of shows for a long time, and I don't remember if there was a mixed audience or not, there may not have been. It may have been only whites down on the floor. But I mean, that whole racial thing was there in society. But music kind of just said, "Screw it." Musicians didn't care about that kind of stuff.

SHORTY NEHRENBERG: I guess that a prime example for me is that we went to the Jazz Festival at Charlotte Coliseum and the Coliseum was full. And the bands played one-by-one, with the Mothers of Invention playing last. So they had a long kind of set up, and so the Mothers were all walking around with long hair and no shirts and fluorescent yo-yo's and there were lots of people everywhere setting up for them. Just kind of chaos. And they finally get up to play a song, and by the end of the second song, the Coliseum had emptied out and there was nobody left in the audience! It went from about twelve thousand people in the audience to about 200 in about fifteen minutes. They all looked at them and heard the music and they just left.

So we sat there and all moved up to watch the show, and it was, to me, technically more advanced than anything we'd seen all night. It was the perfect example of a great jazz setup, it was just wonderful and he'd written every bit of it. It was, to me, just masterful the way he directed everybody. He had little ensembles here and there, three people here, three people there and he'd direct everybody. It was just amazing! It was a great show! I think Lowell George was there. A couple of guys from Little Feat were there. So it was incredible. Well, years later I'm reading Rolling Stone Magazine, and they are interviewing Frank Zappa, and they say to Frank, "Frank, why did you ever break up the Mothers of Invention?" And he said, "Well, one night we were playing in Charlotte, North Carolina, and I realized that the world is not ready for my music, and I decided to quit right then and there." That was the show that we were at.

That is kind of what Charlotte was like to our kind of music. It just didn't even exist! But we were searching for this kind of music because no one else was. In our whole high school there were maybe five of us who really liked this stuff. Everybody else thought we were crazy!

While we were in California, we saw the Youngbloods. Also on that show was a band called The Ultimate Spinach. They were horrible. They were bad. It was like someone was putting a chainsaw to me. And the only reason we stayed was because the Youngbloods were coming on next. And it was like when they finally got off the stage it was like the blue skies just opened up. And Donovan was the final act on this show.

Ultimate Spinach came on and they were just making these god-awful sounds. I found myself getting sick to my stomach. So I went back to those couches that they had set up at the back of the Fillmore, and I sat down next to some man. And I turned to him and said, "Mister, I just took something called LSD. Can you tell me how long it lasts?" And he looked at me and slowly said, "For the rest of your life."

Western and Middle N.C.

DANIEL COSTON: *By 1966, Charlotte bands were touring throughout the state. This included Western North Carolina, where a smattering of venues, and Battle Of The Bands contests were beginning to pop up.*

PAT WALTERS: The Young Ages, I played with a bit. Johnny Barkley had a broken arm, I believe. He'd been in an accident, so he couldn't play, and Rusty was too young to go out much, so I filled in with them. We went up to Appalachian State, or somewhere near Appalachian and played somewhere. They had a bread truck, and about ten of us piled into a bread truck and went up to their gig. And we hiked around up in the mountains. One of the guys said that it was the Linville Gorge. And I had these knee-high moccasins like Hendrix used to wear and they were not good for hiking in the mountains! No support! But, I didn't care!

BOB HINKLE: I got my first guitar when I was six. I was hooked early. There used to be a radio show on WKSY, in Asheville, called "The Sweetcorn Serenade". It was a pretty eclectic show, and I used to sit in my little green rocker, and think, "I want to be involved with that."

In the early 1960s, Asheville was nothing like it is now. It was a fairly sleepy, and a little bit of a redneck town. My secondary motivation with music was, "Well, this might get me out of here." I did love being in the music scene here. I played with a bunch of bands that played two dances, and then went back to real life.

The first band that I was seriously involved with was called the Royal Roulettes, which was to my knowledge, western North Carolina's first racially integrated band. They had two African-American singers, Charles Pickens and Colin Martin. The two of them could not have been more different, but somehow they were great together. Tim Hayden on guitar, Gene Brown on keys, Tim Scofield on drums. I played trumpet in the group. Tim's father opened a restaurant in Asheville, and in the basement they had a jazz club, called the Cave. The place brought in everybody in town.

The Roulettes played the Royal Pines just about every Saturday for almost two years. Because we were an integrated band, we'd play at the Pines from eight to evelen o'clock, and then make the rounds of the African-American clubs. There were a couple of them on Eagle Street. There was a Birdland, where we ended up much of the time. We'd play until 4am, if we could stand it.

When I was in the Roulettes, I was the only one that had access to a car. So I would often take people home at the end of the evening. For about six weeks in a row, I got stopped by the same Asheville police officer, telling me that I was in the wrong neighborhood, at the wrong time. The same lecture, each time. Finally, I said, "If I did something wrong, please pull me over. Otherwise, please don't. I've got professional reasons to be here, which I've stated before." And he left me alone after that, but it was one of the moments when I realized that I had to get out of this place.

At the same time I was playing with the Roulettes, I was enamored of the folk scene. I picked up a number of instruments. My interest in folk was starting to outpace the Roulettes. Eventually, I fell in a couple of other musicians, and we called ourselves the Highlanders. We were basically an acoustic folk trio, so our production values meant that we could play any place, and we often did. Church clubs, corporate events. We were probably best-known for renting out and playing at the Asheville Pavillion, at the Asheville Recreation Park, playing every Saturday night all summer, into the fall. What happened with the Highlanders was what happened with most bands with juniors or seniors. I went off to college, in Chapel Hill.

DANIEL COSTON: *Throughout the 1960s, the music scene throughout western North Carolina began to grow, slowly laying the groundwork for the vibrant scene that is there now.*

BOB HINKLE: Rock and roll bands were around, and people were beginning to get into it. I played with a band at Lee Edwards High School that was more Rock.

DANIEL COSTON: *Garage Rock and psychedelia was slow to spread throughout the state. Much like the Chapel Hill scene for much of the decade, frat-rock and folk-pop bands were in the majority. However, a large scene did emerge from Lee Edwards High School, in Asheville. These bands played popular venues such as the Brown Derby, the Pines, the Sky Club, and the Ozark. Some even ventured into more rough-and-tumble venues like the Hideaway, the Riverboat Lounge, the Amboy Lounge, and the Casa Loma, despite nearly all of the groups still attending high school, and not old enough to legally be in those places.*

The Satyrs were among the first to emerge from Lee Edwards, and were among the most popular. Formed in 1964, the quartet quickly built a following throughout the Asheville area. In 1965, the band recorded their lone single, "Don't Be Surprised"/"Blue Blue World", live on a reel-to-reel recorder at Asheville's High Fidelity Sales store. The

collection of Fabulous Wunz

Fabulous Wunz, 1966.

Satyrs also inspired several of the classmates to also form bands, and record their own songs. In 2013, the members of the Satyrs discovered copies of a one-day, eight song session that they recorded at Marke V Studios in Greenville, SC in 1966. The band is hoping to release these recordings officially in the near future.

The Wunz formed at Lee Edwards in 1965, playing sock hops throughout the area. The following year, the band opened a show for Tommy James & The Shondells at the Civic Center, which is now known as Thomas Wolfe Auditorium. When the Shondells' gear didn't arrive, the band was asked if they would like to rent out their gear to the headliners for that night's show. The Wunz happily offered a higher rental fee, and pocketed the night's extra money. Soon after, the band secured a single deal with Pyramid Records, and recorded their lone single, "If I Cry"/"Please" at Arthur Smith Studios, in Charlotte. The record was credited to the Fabulous Wunz. "If I Cry" went on to be a hit single on Asheville's WISE station, and was number one in Raleigh for several weeks.

With bands like Tommy James & The Shondells, Paul Revere & The Raiders and Sam The Sham & The Pharoahs drawing big crowds at the Civic Center, a local Battle Of The Bands was soon organized. Crowds packed the Civic Center to see several local bands play, but Bee Bumble & The Stingers won the contest with their rendition of "Wipe Out", for which the band's drummer playing the song on the microphone, breaking the mic in the process. The band went on to play shows with Tommy James & The Shondells, Jay & The Techniques, and others.

Other bands at Lee Edwards showcased more R&B, and Soul influences. The Royal Shades played venues throughout the Asheville area from 1964 to 1966. The Shadyz recorded one single with a singer from Shelby named Eddie Holland, who went to regional success in the 1970s under his real name, George Hatcher. The Centurions recorded several singles, though not under their own name. The band recorded for Mercury Records with singer Willie Hobbs as the Dirte Floor, and would later record with Charles Pickens and Billy Mills, who went by the name of Pic And Bill. They also recorded their own LP as the Dirte Floor, entitled Funky Soul, in 1968.

collection of the Ron-De-Voos

Ron-De-Voos, 1966.

While several fine bands in the Asheville area, like the Misfits, never got the chance to record, one band that did record a single was the Ron-De-Voos. Their lone single, featuring the original song "A Trip So Wild", was released in 1967. "A Trip So Wild" is a folk-tinged tale of a possible drug, or love trip gone bad. The song's folkier sound came about when the drums were mixed so low that they became inaudible to most ears, leaving the guitar, bass and its plaintive vocal way out in front.

BOB HINKLE: I saw the Ron-De-Voos on one of my trips back home. I'd come home to visit the family, and you'd want to see what was going on. That was a band that I often heard about when I came back.

DANIEL COSTON: *Asheville also had a TV show that featured some of the new bands in* the area. "The Bob Ledford Show", hosted by the owner of a local used car company, aired on WLOS Channel 13, and hosted a number of bands from the Carolinas.

By the late 1960s, some were also mixing psychedelia in with other musical genres. In 1969, Shirley Hughey released the song "Pink And Green" on the Asheville-based Bandit label. Is it Psychedelic pop? Psychedelic funk? Yes, and yes. The song was included on Ken Friedman's third volume of Tobacco A Go Go, and has been a popular single among collectors for a number of years.

collection of Shirley Hughey

Shirley Hughey, 1974.

The truth behind the "Pink And Green" single is nearly as wild as the song itself. The song was originally performed, and recorded originally by another Asheville-area act, Orange Purple Marmalade. The band was led by Terry and Theresa Justus, with Theresea billed as "Queen Of The Drums." The song, written by fellow bandmember Bob Pruitt, was recorded at Harry Deal's Galaxie III Studios in Taylorsville, NC sometime in 1968. Several months after the session, the studio removed the band's vocals, and had Shirley Hughey, a local singer who was just finishing high school, put a new vocal to the track. The song was released to Asheville radio stations during 1969, and did receive some airplay.

Another Asheville group that carried the new sounds was the Electric Love, who released two fine singles as the decade ended. Another group, the Looking Glass, represented North Carolina at that year's national Battle Of The Bands competition, which was held in Raleigh. One local paper at the time featured photos of the band waving as they boarded the plane to Raleigh, looking much like a certain British band that had arrived on American shores just a few years before. The Looking Glass finished fourth.

Bands from Charlotte were also playing in the "Tobacco Road" portion of North Carolina, which made up much of the central portion of the state. One of the most active areas in the state for the new sounds was the Winston-Salem and Greensboro areas. In 1964, rock and roll bands began to emerge alongside the beach music and R&B bands that had been in vogue. Along with these bands, new record labels also began to pop up. Yet not all record labels were what they originally seemed.

TIM TATUM: The Stowaways played a lot of Battle of the Bands, which were popular at the time. We did a Battle of the Bands at Catawba College, and came in second. After the show, a guy from Justice Records came backstage and said, "How'd you guys like to record for us?" Little did we know that it would cost $800.

DANIEL COSTON: Calvin Newton began Justice Records in 1965, and was based in Winston-Salem. Justice was essentially a "pay to play" label. For eight hundred dollars, the band would an entire album during one day of studio time. Photos for the album were also taken the same day as the recording session. The artist would receive 500 copies of their album, which they could then sell as they pleased. Eight hundred dollars was a lot of money at the time, especially for parents that may not have wanted their kids

collection of Daniel Coston
1969 National Battle of the Bands program.

to spend this kind of money on this passing youthful fad. However, in a time when time in a recording studio was out of reach of most bands, the chance to record a full-length album was something that many bands did jump at. This included soul, R&B, surf-

rock and beach music bands from North Carolina such as the Bonnevilles, Nightriders, Variations and the Generations Combo, as well as more garage rock-inclined bands such as the Speculations, Varcels, Starliters, and the Stowaways.

KEN KNIGHT: We did everything in one six, seven hour block. One take for everything, vocals done live. It was hard to stay in tune. There was one song that we did more than once. It starts off with this bullfrog voice of "You lie," and I couldn't do it right. Eventually, the engineer came down, and that's who you hear on the record.

TIM TATUM: One of the most frustrating things with the fact that we couldn't hear what was going on. You couldn't hear yourself singing, because everything was so loud. Our amps were over in one corner.

KEN KNIGHT: They only had one pair of earphones for the drummer, and a couple of us were alongside one wall, and the others were along the other. The one-day block didn't really allow much beyond one take. There were two guys in the control room. They'd play it back, and they'd say, "Well, we've got that one." The photos for the album were also done the same day as the session. After the session, we listened to it on one of our parents' Hi-Fi, and we just wanted to do it again.

DENNIS EDWARDS: The band that I was in at the time played some original songs. I remember writing two or three songs. We had a deal. The Stowaways cut their record, and we packed up a little U-Haul trailer and drove up to Winston-Salem and auditioned for that same record company. And they said, "Oh yeah, we'll cut you an album, but it'll cost you $800!" We came back all fired up and ready to go. But that was $200 per parent, and they weren't about to do it. We would have had a record on that same label. That's why we were so dashed when we found out we wouldn't get to record ours. We had the contract but couldn't get the money to do it. We tried. We had a big meeting, but we didn't get unanimous consent.

DANIEL COSTON: *Justice Records was only part of a thriving scene in Winston-Salem. The Teen-Beats formed in Winston-Salem at the end of 1964. Over the next three years, the quartet released two singles, with the first recorded in Charlotte at Arthur Smith Studios. The band's first single, "I Guess That's Why You're Mine"/"Not In Love With Me", received a good amount of airplay in Winston-Salem, and the band got further attention by dying their hair beet red, to match their name. In 1967, the band renamed themselves the Words Of Luv. They signed with Hickory Records to release* *a new single, "I'd Have To Be Outta My Mind"/"Tommorow's A Long Time", and toured throughout the region before breaking up in 1967. Other Winston-Salem bands that released singles during this time include the Rockets Combo, Speculations, and Sounds Unlimited.*

The town of Concord, near Charlotte yielded numerous bands during the 1960s. Bands such as the Tamrons, Huns, Phantom Raiders, the Ravens, Fantastik Four, West Wind, the Swinging Sensations, and the Surfmates. Many of these groups played at the local Green Dragon teen club, as well as other venues.

The Tamrons released "Wild Man", backed with "Stop Look Listen", in 1966 at Arthur Smith Studios. The band had originally planned to release another song, entitled "Genie." During a Tamrons practice, the quintet got a visit from the Huns. The Huns heard "Genie" at the practice, and soon after rush-recorded and released their own version of "Genie," which they also re-titled as "Shakedown". The Tamrons went to the Huns' house to confront the group, but were turned away by the Huns' manager, who was the father of some of the bandmembers.

Despite that incident, both the Tamrons and the Huns shared the same record label. Pyramid Records was owned by Arthur Smith, and released several singles from various North Carolina groups. This included Greensboro-based bands like the King Bees. The label also released 45s by Carolina-based groups such as the Londons, Eradicators, and the Charlotte-based Damascans.

TONI FIELDS: The Damascans was the first band that I played in. My brother was in the Damascans, and when they first started they always practiced at my house. It was just kind of a natural progression since we were the house with the music room and several instruments.

Buddy Hyman was about 19 when we started [the Damascans]. He is the person who wrote the songs on the 45 we did, "Go Way Girl" and "Diane". I believe the song "Diane" was about his girlfriend. He was a student at UNCC and, sadly, in 1968 he was killed in a murder/suicide out at UNCC. Another student shot him because Buddy was dating a girl who had dated the other student. Really tragic. We did the 45 in '66, and he was killed in '68, so that was the end of the band.

Buddy lived next door to Arthur Smith, so that is how we got hooked up with him to do the 45. We recorded the single at Arthur Smith's studio. We were fortunate to have the connection with Lanny Smith and Buddy. I remember playing a Hammond B-3 that was in the studio, and Arthur being in the studio with us.

[My other bandmates were] Lanny Smith, Arthur's nephew, was our manager. Other bandmates were my brother, David Naples (drums), who can play many instruments and still plays in bands to this day. Jackie Holmes played bass. At times, we had a singer, Scott Pope. They were all in high school, except Buddy.

DANIEL COSTON: *You were a rarity in that were a female in what was largely a male-dominated scene. And a young lady, at that. Did you ever have any trouble with that? Did some people give you a hard time?*

collection of Toni Fields

The Damascans, 1966.

TONI NAPLES: It was different being a female in a band back then. I think I had to work a lot harder to be taken seriously. I was really young, only 13, so my brother was charged with taking care of me. My dad was involved with the band, so he went to most of the gigs. I don't think my brother was really excited about having to look after me.

DANIEL COSTON: *The Tymes Syndicate Band formed in Albemarle, NC in 1967, out of the remains of two local bands, Winter's Children, and DC & the Daytonas. The seven-member band, led by vocalist Bernie Harris, were largely influenced by the beach music sounds of the region, but did incorporate some of the newer Rock & Roll sounds into their show. The group toured the region, eventually establishing themselves at The Beach Party club, in Myrtle Beach, SC. Their lone single, "An Uphill Climb"/"Change My Direction", was released nationally by ABC Records. Another band that mined the same garage/soul/beach territory as the Tymes Syndicate was the Kallabash Corporation, who were based in Greensboro. In 1970, the band released a full-length album on the tiny Uncle Bill label.*

The Revised Edition were a four-piece band that formed in Asheboro in 1968, and released their lone single, "Thoughts"/"Illusions Of You", in 1969. The Changin' Tymes, from Morganton, released one single and appeared on Dick Clark's "Happening" TV

collection of Mitch Easter

Sacred Irony, 1969.

show. Other groups in the central North Carolina area that recorded singles during this time included the Martians (from Hickory), Turks (from Elkin), and the Nomads (Mount Airy).

One single from this area that has gained attention amongst collectors is "Boot-Leg"/"Whatzit?" The single was recorded by the IV Pak, who were from Ruffin, NC. In 1967, the band traveled to Danville, VA to record at House Of Sound Studios. The group, who were actually the VI Pack, recorded the R&B-infused instrumental "Boot-Leg" as the intended A-side. When the producer what the B-side was, the band quickly came up with a "Psychotic Reaction" influenced Garage rave-up, and gave it the title "Whatzit?" When the single was released on Raven Records offshoot Hippie Records, the VI Pack had been switched to IV Pak.

Let's return to Winston-Salem, a scene that included popular bands such as the Eradicators, the Vee Jays, and the Clique, which featured Chuck Dale Smith, and local guitar hero Sam Moss. In the midst of all these bands, a new group of musicians would soon emerge to change how the North Carolina music scene would be seen by the rest of the world. Chris Stamey, Peter Holsapple, Will Rigby, and others would all come up in Winston-Salem's music scene in the late 1960s and early '70s. One of the groups that propelled the Winston-Salem scene during that time was Sacred Irony, whose song "I See Love" got airplay on two local stations, WAIR and WOTB, in 1969. Mitch Easter, who is still an in-demand guitarist, writer and record producer, began his career as part of Sacred Irony.

DANIEL COSTON: *When did you start playing music?*

MITCH EASTER: I took trumpet in Junior High, and I was not too good! Later I switched to Baritone Horn, because I had braces and these instruments have bigger mouthpieces, for less pain! And I really liked the Baritone Horn, or Euphonium, but by then I think I was already on the Road to Ruin, because I started playing guitar when I was twelve.

DANIEL COSTON: *How much effect did the Beatles on Ed Sullivan, and the British Invasion have on you?*

MITCH EASTER: It was huge! I was one of those kids who would sit through the juggling acts waiting for the rock band. My parents took me and a friend to see "A Hard Day's Night" when it came to Winston-Salem, at the Flamingo Drive-In. That night, we tried to record something! We were terrible, of course. We went to that movie as "kids" and returned as "aspiring Rock musicians"! It was that powerful. Almost all the bands seemed great, at that time.

DANIEL COSTON: *How did you find new music, and new bands?*

MITCH EASTER: We had two Top 40 AM radio stations here that were pretty cool for a long time. You'd go to somebody's basement and hear their new LP, which was always exciting. For example, the Dodson brothers had a cool basement floor in their house, which was like the Boys' Apartment, and they always had the latest sounds. I think I first heard the Who's Tommy, and Led Zeppelin I down there. Later, my friend Chris Stamey seemed to buy everything and I heard important milestones like Shazam, by the Move, at his house.

DANIEL COSTON: *Describe your first band, and first show.*

MITCH EASTER: My first band was called The Loyal Opposition, and the first show was at Floretta Baylin's Dance Academy, a teen dance, in the fall of '67. Everybody wanted us to do "Incense and Peppermints", and we didn't know it! Oops. This was Showbiz Lesson Number One, I guess. You have to know the latest sounds! The band was me on rhythm guitar, Doug Muir on lead guitar, and Robin Borthwick on drums. We had matching clothes, featuring double-breasted blazers. We were at least three years out of date with this look. We should have been more psychedelic, obviously! Later, this band got a guy named Bobby, who sang and played organ, which expanded the sound a lot. Still no bass, we just had the bass keys on the organ. But that was an improvement, anyway.

DANIEL COSTON: *What was music scene like in Winston-Salem? Were there a lot of bands?*

MITCH EASTER: Yes, loads. Lots of "soul bands" setups based on the Memphis sound, a Rock band plus horns. Then there were two notable psychedelic bands, Captain Speed and His Fungi Electric Mothers, and Mr. Glasspak and His Magic Mufflers. Both were glorious. Mr. Glasspak was notable in being a duo! Mac Chambers played organ and guitar, and he had a console organ, instead of the usual Farfisa, or other "combo" organ. I still marvel at the fact that they did "Hope For Happiness", by Soft Machine. Captain Speed were huge here, and a truly great band.

DANIEL COSTON: *Did your classmates, and teachers look at you differently for being in a band?*

MITCH EASTER: For me, it was an escape from the concerns of Junior High social life, which was great, because it was getting really unpleasant and not my cup of tea by the time I met Sam Moss, who was my entre into something altogether more serious with this music stuff. Once I'd played with Sam, I just thought about Hendrix all the time, and knew that it did not matter about alpaca sweaters and stupid kid social cliques! What a relief.

DANIEL COSTON: *How did the Imperturbable Teutonic Griffin come about?*

MITCH EASTER: That was the band that was formed when Sam asked me and Robin Borthwick to join him and Corky McMillan in a new situation. Sam saw The Loyal Opposition at Knollwood (Church) Coffeehouse, and I guess he thought Robin and I had some potential.

DANIEL COSTON: *How did that turn into Sacred Irony?*

MITCH EASTER: After Sam left the ITG, we carried on a bit with me attempting to take over on "lead" guitar. With a few personnel shifts, we became Sacred Irony. The main thing is that at some point we went to doing all original songs. This was a pretty bold move when most bands were cover bands, and I think I was a driving force behind this. I thought, if you want to make records, well, you need to have your own songs. But I didn't really know how to write songs, and the best ones were written by Dale Smith and Corky McMillan. We stayed pretty popular, though, which was most encouraging. We did open for the Yellow Payges a couple of times, and they were awesome! And then we got the gig of being the backing band for Bobby Sherman when he played in Winston-Salem. That was pretty great.

DANIEL COSTON: *What happened to Sacred Irony?*

MITCH EASTER: I was the youngest one in the band, and at a certain point the rest of the band wanted to go back to doing covers. I think this was because they were ready to Make It with the Ladies, and back then everybody thought that the pinnacle was playing The Pavillion, in Myrtle Beach, SC. I think the other guys thought they could learn "Whipping Post," get booked at the Pavillion, and meet girls. I was the idealist, who thought that going back to covers was a sellout! So I quit, which was totally heartbreaking for me. The band got Ed Dodson in on guitar to replace me, and they worked up their covers and carried on for a while.

DANIEL COSTON: *What do you think about, when you think about that time in your life?*

MITCH EASTER: I feel fortunate to have gotten to play in bands that long ago. It was such a different time, but it was invaluable for gaining confidence as a musician and of course I feel like I have a deeper perspective on things as a result. My background is so different from people playing now! And yet in a way, it's always the same. I suppose some of my stories are really funny to younger people!

CHAPTER EIGHT
1967, a Changing Scene

JAKE BERGER: Known for the infamous "Summer Of Love", 1967 really was something, just not what is commonly supposed. It started out in the early spring or late winter as media hype encouraging people, to make the "trip" to San Francisco where, according to them, there was a host of "beautiful people" waiting there with "flowers in their hair" for all of us with nothing on their minds except the desire to "make love not war" with us, and to "get back to a simpler time" and about every other catch phrase that a pack of hackneyed reporters could conjure up. Nothing mattered to them but the opportunity to create more "copy" in order to sell, sell, sell, more rags. This was not restricted to newsprint, either. There was always some blip on the news about the strange goings on "out there" in the land of weird.

What in reality had started in the 1950s as a bohemian "beat culture" of artists, writer, filmmakers, and the just plain too odd to fit in anywhere else, had by now become so large a phenomenon, spurred on by the advent of the new music and surplus of baby-boomers that had become disillusioned with the status quo, that the original inhabitants of that particular murky social scene had either cut and run long ago, or were gearing up for a quick exodus. What had started as a good, overly idealistic idea, quickly degenerated as every dis-enfranchised kid in the country made their way to the promised land, Height-Ashbury. And come they did, in spades.

The Haight very rapidly filled with young, mostly teenaged kids who arrived without a penny to their name or any idea as to how to sustain themselves. They quickly became immersed in drug addiction. Crystal methadrine flooded the market, along with poorly made acid with suspect ingredients. Along with the curious, dis-enfranchised kids, bums, hobos, the insane, runaways, and thrill seekers, came the predators. Even serial killer Charles Manson was there, assembling his crew of followers. In hindsight, I'm glad I didn't make the trek. Far away from the gaudy circus that was 'Frisco, there was certainly a "vibe" present that summer, even here in Charlotte.

I spent the whole summer on my own. Things had gotten so bad at home, that I just opted to stay away for the duration of the summer. I spent that time wandering from place to place, staying where I could. At this point, I should thank the mother of a friend from the shopping center, where we would hang. His mom seemed to understand what was happening at my house, and after a call to my mom, I ended up there for a short while before moving on to new environs. Between the "shopping center posse" and the kids that I made music with, I had plenty of things to keep me busy.

The songs that were played the most on the radio that summer? "Let's Live For Today," by the Grass Roots, "Brown Eyed Girl", by Van Morrison, "Ode To Billy Joe" by Bobby Gentry, "Light My Fire" by the Doors, and "A Whiter Shade Of Pale" from Procol Harum! Also that summer, as everyone knows, Sgt. Pepper was released and almost single handedly turned the singles market, and music in general upside down. "Strawberry Fields" was released as a teaser to the album and a friend of mine, Mary Ann Samples, had stated that the Beatles were breaking up, and you could hear it in the music. Well, maybe a year off, but she was correct. They were tired of being Beatles by 1968. That spring, you could have hardly turned the radio on without being assailed by "Penny Lane", and by the end of the summer, the money-making machine dumped an ersatz musical group that had their own TV show. Hey Hey! We all became fans of the Monkees!

DANIEL COSTON: *Some will put the fisrt of June in 1967 down as the day that psychedelia was unleashed on the world. That day's release of the new Beatles album, entitled Sgt. Pepper's Lonely Hearts Club Band, signaled to the mainstream world that the times had indeed changed. However, the album was in many ways a two-way mirror. The album reflected what the Beatles saw happening around them, as much as it showed the band's own state of mind. Rock & Roll had begun to talk about more than what was happening at that moment. It was making suggestions of the future, and what was possible.*

STEVE STOECKEL: Around here, up to then, the music had been Rhythm & Blues, beach music. A little bit of rockabilly, but also country music. All of a sudden, these were the driving forces behind younger people, and what they're going out to hear. Beach music bands were still going strong, but then this new music was cutting into that. All these kids brought all this music in, and this is what was going on.

DONNY FLETCHER: The music was great, because it was all so much. First you heard the Stones, and then you heard the Small Faces. Meanwhile, you're still trying to learn "Wipe Out". Where was this music coming from?

DANIEL COSTON: *After a few years of learning to play the guitar, Zan McLeod had joined the Die Hards, a band that shared rehearsal space with local musician Pat Carpenter.*

ZAN MCLEOD: The Die Hards practiced in Pat's basement all the time. And from there, there were about half a dozen musicians around the neighborhood who used to hang out there. And then I moved to South in the 11th grade. I went to Olympic in the 10th grade.

I played with The Die Hards at the dances, the Christmas dance and maybe a spring one, too. It was kind of weird for me because I knew everybody at Olympic because it was a brand new school, and then when I moved to South, I didn't know anybody!

But I immediately started going to The Web. I kept going to The Web, and I met people over there. And they were some of the people who lived in my neighborhood. There was a guy named Charlie, who lived in a house with a music room in it. He had a soul band. When I moved into the neighborhood, I heard the music. So I went down there and knocked on the door and introduced myself and started playing with them. They also played at The Web.

JAKE BERGER: Zan played with the Durations, after I was with them. Even then, Zan was really good.

DEBBY DOBBINS: I remember the Purple Penguin, on Central Avenue. That was around 1967 or 1968. That's when I met Zan McLeod. We were each other's first love. We still communicate by email. And my parents used to say, "That boy has long hair and he'll never amount to anything!" So it was really fun to show them the pictures of him playing at The White House at Laura Bush's birthday party! He's a special person. A really talented guitarist. I remember going with him to his gigs and he'd be playing the solo for "Crossroads" note-for-note, and I'd be so proud!

DANIEL COSTON: *The year was a busy one for the Paragons, who were still riding the wave of their "Abba" single, and arriving at shows in a custom-painted hearse.*

ZAN MCLEOD: Oh yeah, they were like Rock stars! They had groupies, they had outfits. Each guy had his own kind of "look" and they were influenced by the Beatles, that Sgt. Pepper look. I think that they had some military coats, and stuff like that. They were taking that psychedelic edge that no one else around here dared to do at the time, or even knew about. I mean people just didn't know, I mean, I barely knew what it was! I was like, "What the hell is this?" We'd only seen pictures in magazines of it.

DANIEL COSTON: *The way that the Paragons presented themselves made many kids in the area want to do the same, although their parents did not always share the same enthusiasm.*

BOBBY DONALDSON: We got a hearse for our band. I just remember the hearse only lasted a short amount of time. My mom told me, "You can't. You will not ride in that hearse." My parents told me that I could go anywhere I wanted and I could play with anyone I wanted to play with, as long as I didn't get into any trouble! But they would not let me ride in that hearse! I mean, that was just the thing! "You ain't gonna have nothing to do with no hearse, and no coffin."

ZAN MCLEOD: Pat Walters was by far the best. He was like five years ahead of everybody else. I don't know how he did it. He studied the Blues records. He was by far the best around! He was really out there with how he looked back in those days! He was really tall and skinny with really long curly hair. I mean, he just looked like a real guitar-player! He really did. He was world-class. He could play as good as Clapton.

DANNY HUNTLEY: I remember a large Battle Of The Bands, the largest I can recall, being at A.L. Brown (Kannapolis) High School auditorium, which was a rather large stage and seating arrangement. We won that, and launched us as sort of the best around.

After "Abba" came out, and as we polished up on a number of hit songs of the time, we played in many places, more particularly the Statesville Armory several times. The Web, a dance place for teens in bottom of the YMCA on Morehead, many times. A friend of the band from Chesterfield, SC, her dad was a prominent citizen, and we had multiple bookings at the Chesterfield National Guard Armory. The Park Center, behind Memorial Stadium in Charlotte, we also had several bookings there. There most probably were many other places, but these come to mind. The pinnacle of our success was our manager arranged for us to be third billing at the 1966 New Year's Eve Party at the original Charlotte Coliseum behind The Hollies and the top billing, Herman's Hermits. We were supposed to meet them, according to our manager, but that never came to pass. It was quite an exciting night playing before a Coliseum full of people, and we were popular enough locally, we were very well received. We may have played the flip side to "Abba", "Better Man Than I", by the Yardbirds, before actually playing "Abba".

JAKE BERGER: I went to a Band Battle at Park Road Shopping Center. The Paragons won, of course, but something that has always remained in memory is the purest form of garage band I have ever seen. The group was a north Charlotte group from Hawthorne Junior High, and they were named the Penetrations. The two main players in this band were guitarist Henry Bigham and faux bassist Freddy Windham. The Penetrations had no bassist, and Freddy would play the bass parts on his guitar until time for the solo and then would fire off a scalding solo before reverting back to the bass pattern. Can you get any more garage than that? I defy you to not agree. And that's not to say that they were any good, but just that do it yourself ethos that has always been the back bone of that form and that frame of mind extended to its descendent, punk rock, and is still evident in young music to this day.

BOBBY DONALDSON: I was going to Myers Park by that point. For me, it really didn't change that much! Because I was usually not there on Mondays and Fridays. On Mondays, I was not there because I had been out on a gig all weekend, and Fridays because I had to leave early, to go to the gig. I never went to dances. I never got to do any of that. Because I was always playing at somebody else's place, and traveling around. We were like the Hit Attractions band back then.

DOUG JAMES: The first time that I ever heard Jimi Hendrix, I thought, "Oh, my God!" you know, and it, everything in my life, at that time certainly, even when I was still 14. It was still every decision I made was about what was the next musical thing I'm gonna do? When is the next rehearsal, when is the next gig?

You know how when a guy is a year or two older than you, and he's not always real nice to you? Well, Boyd Albritton always was nice. Boyd was always decent to me and showed me stuff. Like, "You ought to try thin strings", stuff like that. And he had an awesome Les Paul Custom. Boyd is the one who gave me the recommendation that took me away. I got the call from the Aqualads and they said, "Boyd Albritton said that we should call you." And I was like, "Cool," and that was it! There was no turning back at that point. I was 15.

My dad tried to "buy me out" of it, at that point. Before I went out on that first road trip, he offered me money not to do it. I owed him some money for some equipment that I'd bought, and he was concerned about my safety and well-being. But having said that I thought, "What's the point of me having all that stuff if I'm not gonna go use it?"

JAKE BERGER: Well, you chose your path long before that.

DOUG JAMES: Well, it kind of chose me.

BOYD ALBRITTON: I made the band, the Noblemen, wear suits. Because we got more gigs, and we made money. I always wanted to play with a better band. It all was a stepping stone thing, with me. I wanted to make more money, I wanted to play with better bands, and I wanted better guitars.

collection of Boyd Albritton

The Noblemen, 1966.

JAKE BERGER: One night that spring, I went to Camp Thunderbird (the Boy Scout's camp, on the Catawba River) with a friend from down the street. His name was Gerald Burgess, and his father was a police officer. We used to run around together, getting up to all sorts of harmless mischief. There was a band playing at the camp, and when we got there I realized it was a conglomeration of the Abbadons, and the Paragons. There was Gaines Brown (who is now a very successful graphic artist) on bass, and Larry Duckworth drumming, both from the Abbadons. Dave Long, who I had seen playing the folk tents at the Festival In The Park on guitar and harmonica, and then there was Pat Walters, his guitar painted with colorful "op art" designs and that ungodly mound of funky assed hair.

This was the spring before hippies, and while the styles were most certainly going in that direction, it hadn't gotten there yet, but there was Pat, a most freaky looking dude. If you knew him though, you would see a perfectly well mannered young man who was probably the least wild child you'd ever want to meet. I thought this was a new band on the scene, because they were so skilled, but they were just a "throw together band" assembled for the one gig. There were a ton of one-off gigs with any number of combinations, from different combos that would take a gig just to be out there playing, in those days.

Later that summer, there was another Battle Of The Bands held at Freedom Park. As I was hanging around looking to see what i could get into, up pulls a hearse, painted in what would shortly be termed "psychedelic" artwork. It was the Paragons, and they were not just showing up for a gig, they were making a statement. Keeping in mind that hair had not been that long as a norm for about 200 years, you can imagine the impression made on the unsuspecting people that were gathered in the park that day. Dressed in the most outlandish assortment of Nehru jackets, brocade, and robes, Edwardian

collection of Larry Duckworth

Larry's Sound Department, 1967.

velvet and bedecked with (literally) flowers in their hair, I knew that the Mothership had landed! The Paragons played their set ("We Ain't Got Nothin' Yet", "Walk Away Renee", and of course, "Abba") with Pat Walters standing stone still, resplendent in a Myers Park band uniform, complete with the tall "plumed" band hat. (I heard later that the person that lent it to him got kicked out of the orchestra.)

Then they were replaced on the stage with an up and coming group from the south side called the Modulation Blooze, which featured a too tall guitarist, Shorty Nehrenberg, frontman Dennis Edwards, and the old drummer from the Barons, Phil Lowe. Pat sat in with the Mod-Blooze as well, doing "Smokestack Lightning", and "Born In Chicago" by the Butterfield Blues Band. There was also the old Abbadons with a new lineup, and new name. They were now to be known as Larry's Sound Department. (Get it?) There also was a newer band dubbed The Young Ages, from north Charlotte, with an uncanny knack for playing Animals songs and sounding scary close to the originals, and then a group from Statesville, NC, called the Cast.

This was the first Battle Of The Bands that I had been to in which the Paragons didn't win. The unknown Cast did, and they should have, as they were many notches above the local heroes on the skill stick. They did the Bar-Kays' "Soul Finger", and a song titled "New York Mining Disaster 1941" by the brand new Bee Gees. For those that think of "disco music" when the Bee Gees' name is mentioned, I would strongly suggest that you check out the stuff they were doing in the mid 1960s, as I know you will be surprised at the quality of neo-psychedelic and Beatlesque material they were doing at that time.

collection of Shorty Nehrenberg

The Modulation Blues Band at The Web, 1967.

So this whole day was an eye opening experience for me. One reason is the fact that the barriers of "You can only play as a member of One Band At A Time" shattered for me that day. The other is all of a sudden you could express yourself through your manner of dress as flamboyantly as you could, with the only restriction being your imagination, and it was okay. Within reason, of course. There was beginning to be an air of something new and different, just getting ready to happen. Though you were not quite sure what it was, you just could feel the excitement in the air. As the Buffalo Springfield sang a few months later, "Something's happening here".

DANIEL COSTON: *In the summer of 1967, Shorty Nehrenberg and Dennis Edwards had joined forces with former Barons drummer Phil Lowe to form the Modulation Blooze Band.*

SHORTY NEHRENBERG: It was more of a matter of how to piece equipment together, as in, someone's got an amp, and I got a guitar, now we need to get the drums together. I guess Phil Lowe had the drums, and Dave Clark had the bass. So it was like, "Who has a bass, and who has the guitar?" We really didn't know a whole lot about what we were doing. Phil was the most accomplished one, for sure.

We were just trying to get a couple of noises that would fit together and kind of get it all together piece-by-piece. We hoped that it kind of sounded like we envisioned with the new stuff, because we never had any misconceptions that we were any great musicians or anything. It was hard to learn that stuff, back then.

JAKE BERGER: Two of the more interesting cats that turned up were really more of a team, Shorty Nehrenberg and Dennis Edwards. Shorty and Dennis were then, and still are great friends who though I thought were maybe a year older, but in reality were two or three years older. So they had much further progressed on the "worldly scale", and as musicians.

At the time, I thought that they were like me and my contemporaries, and had picked up the music torch by the influence of the Brit bands that were still dominating the charts (though America had been fighting back for a year or two, by now), but as I found out later they had actually been indoctrinated into the whole shebang via the folk music scene.

My introduction to them came from their frequent appearances at the shopping center, but the thing that left the lasting impression was the fact that even though they were older (back then a year or two really made the difference on the social scene), they were always cordial and there was many a time Shorty would pick me up while hitch-hiking and sometimes discuss the latest by the Stones or Yardbirds. Me the kid acting "grown up", and Shorty in his fringed buckskin jacket (they would become massively popular a few years later), tooling about town in his mid-60s Buick Skylark.

Later, and this just might be urban rumor, but it still sounds good today, their choral teacher at South Meck asked Dennis what was on the agenda for the summer of '67. Dennis informed him that he and Shorty were headed to San Francisco, and here's where the story gets cool. The teacher then asks him "Why?" to which Dennis replies, "Man, everything is happening out there!" I don't know if this is true or not, but it sounds great.

WOODY WILLIAMS: Our band, Fragmentary Blue, was psychedelic. We were influenced by Hendrix. We thought that the Beatles were too pop, or "Fiddle-dee-dee," as we used to say. We would play "Gloria" for 25 minutes. We played Wesley's, which was a club out on Tryon Street. We played there once with the Paragons. We played some other places, as well as a lot of private parties. We got harassed a lot at Garinger High for having long hair. I got pulled over so many times, just for having long hair. When I went into the Army in 1968, that broke up the band.

DANIEL COSTON: *David Floyd also found himself in a new group in 1967.*

DAVID FLOYD: So, a few of the members that it wasn't time for them to go to college, they were still a year away, they got the three of us that were left over from the Gaylords and they put together a band that was called The Flares. And that's when I started playing R&B. Up until then it was kind of an English rock and roll thing. The Beatles were our inspiration. We had three girls up front, that was the thing about the Flares. We had three cute girls up front doing all the Marvelettes-type things, and the Supremes things like that.

We played with the Flares until 1970. And some of the guys that hadn't gone to school yet, from The Counts who were still with us, decided that it was time to leave and head off to college and some of the girls left, too.

collection of David Floyd

The Flares, 1967.

DANIEL COSTON: *By 1967, the Grifs were on the road full-time, and getting ready to release their next single.*

BARRY STACKS: With both of our singles, the eventual A-Side hadn't been the plan. "Catch A Ride" wasn't meant to be the A-Side, until after the session was over. After the session, there was no question. This was the side. When we up traveling in the Midwest, Arnie took us into a studio in Detroit, and we recorded "Keep Dreaming", and "Northbound." "Northbound" is very autobiographical, in that it's about a band going north, playing guitars. We didn't know what side to release. It was Arnie that decided to release "Northbound" as a single. He liked the horns in it. He was a real Soul guy. He went into this nightclub that he used to frequent, and somebody had put our new single on the jukebox there. And while he was there, he realized that he'd made a mistake, because all night long, people kept going up to the jukebox and playing "Keep Dreaming". But by the time that record was released, the Grifs were no more.

We were getting ready to record an album that summer, and our drummer left the band to go back to Charlotte. He was going back to pharmacy school. He didn't see any future in this. Whereas the rest of us, we thought that was what we were supposed to be doing, and that we were on our way. We couldn't believe it in when he just packed up and said, "Well, I gotta go. I have to start school in a few days, in Charlotte." Are you out of your mind?

ROY SKINNER: I had been offered a scholarship to this school, and I would lose it if I didn't take it. I had told them that I was planning on doing this, so I headed back home. Mike Wingate had also just received his draft notice.

BARRY STACKS: That was the beginning of the downfall. As much as my songwriting was a part of the Grifs, his beat was the sound of the Grifs. We auditioned a few guys, and nothing really clicked. The jobs started to dry up, and Bobby and Mike headed back to Charlotte. I'd heard that the music scene was really happening in California, so I headed out to California.

DANIEL COSTON: *By the end of 1966, Rob Thorne was out of the Catalinas, and had fully immersed himself in his new band, the 18th Edition. By the end of the year, the band would become the only Charlotte Rock & Roll band of the 1960s to record a full-length album for a major label. The band's album, by which time they had been renamed the New Mix, came out on United Artists Records in 1968.*

DEBBY DOBBINS: When they were gonna play a show, they'd catch the bus over to my uncle's gas station on Hawthorne, and then pick Rob up. It was always, "I wonder what Rob is gonna be today?" He was like Madonna! He kept re-inventing himself!

ROB THORNE: In '66, maybe '67, Johnny Barker, and I think Tommy Garner, and others would go out and play schools. One thing we did was, we'd go to these schools around the region. We'd take a Beatles song and we would do it in different musical styles. Like in an assembly, for musical education things that we used to do.

We'd do a Beatles song like "I Wanna Hold Your Hand", or something like that, or any of them, and we'd do it in country style or bluegrass style, or a jazz style or R&B style, or something like that to show them that that one song could be done in so many different ways. And then, during that period, after we'd been doing that for a while, in maybe '66 or '67, I met David Brown of the New Mix. Dave had been playing sax with a band, and I met him at The Cellar. He was also a guitar player, only I didn't know that.

I think I met him in '66 or '67, when he came back from France. He'd gone to France for a couple of years to write and be a poet, and he'd married a French girl and brought her back, and he was living in Statesville up the street from Tommy. And I went up there one day, and I met him. And I think that Johnny Barker was up there, and he was a Beatle nut, he was just crazy about The Beatles, and by then I was really just getting into the Beatles stuff and that whole British Rock & Roll thing.

So, Johnny Barker, Tommy Garner from the Catalinas and I, and David Brown and I, put together a quartet and we'd go out and play Beatles, British invasion stuff and a few things like that. We got good at it, and we recorded a couple of singles on Panther Records. Up at a radio station in Statesville. And all of a sudden, David and I were just hooked on this sound, and I didn't want to play with the Catalinas anymore!

So we tried to talk Johnny Barker and Tommy Garner into leaving the Catalinas and joining us in this quartet, and try to really record some stuff. But they decided not to, and they stayed where they were. I had been living with Gary Barker. Johnny's brother had a trailer park in Statesville, so I moved from there into David Brown's house. I moved in there and they had a practice house out back, there was a foam-padded, soundproof practice room, and David played guitar at that time, and we needed a piano player. Henry Steele, who was with Good Bad And The Ugly later on, was one of the Brown family's friends from High School and he was a regular who hung out at that Davis house. We were mentioning that we needed a piano player and a bass player, and that we were trying to put this thing together. And he said, "I play piano a little bit, classical piano." So all of a sudden, we had three! David started writing stuff, Henry started writing stuff. That's the only band I ever sang with. I sang all the Tenor parts on all the New Mix stuff.

So then we needed a bass player, because Tommy Garner had played bass with us in that first incarnation of this group. And I think that we called the group the 18th Edition, initially. Even when Tommy and Johnny were there. So we were looking for a bass-player and we advertised in the Charlotte paper and this guy answered our ad. His name was Karl Jarvi, and so we invited him up for an audition, and he showed up there one day in a Checker Cab. That's what he drove, a Checker cab, and he had everything he owned in that car. Everything. He moved out of his parents house and he moved to Statesville and we were thinking, "Well now, this is only an audition, so why did you bring everything that you own up here? What if we don't want you in the band?"

So we had an audition and he played for probably about five minutes and we said, "Okay! This is good, you're in the band!" He said that he was confident that he was gonna get the job! That's why he brought everything with him. And almost immediately we had a band! And we started jamming and writing songs. David would stay up sometimes all night, and the next morning we would all get together over coffee and he'd sit there and play all these songs that he'd written the night before. It was just amazing how much great music David Brown was cranking out! He was inspired and he was on fire, and a lot of the influences were Beatlesque, but a lot were not.

We started playing little gigs around different places like that, we were still called The 18th Edition. Panther Records was the local label up in Statesville that this guy named Joe Beaver owned. Joe and his sister and his brother-in-law owned a string of haircutting salons, called Hairstyles Inc., or something like that. It was a big deal up there at the time in that section of the state.

We decided that we actually wanted to record a real album, so I called my uncle, Les Brown, and told him about the band. So he said, "Send a demo out to me". So I did. I sent him one of the wax demos or whatever they were, and about a week later he called me up and said, "Can you guys go to New York next weekend?" And I said, "Yeah, why?" And he said, "Because I've arranged for you to record with Glenn Osser. And you need to call Glenn today, and go ahead and put it in the works. And Glenn Osser, during the Big Band days was one of the most famous arrangers. His real name is Abe Osser, but they called him Glenn. He arranged for most of the big bands. He did most of the arrangements for Les Brown for years. And there were some other guys. Billy Rollins, who was a piano player who arranged was one, also.

So we struck a deal and went up there, I think the next weekend or two weeks later, something like that. We got a trailer and put all our stuff in it, and showed up in New York at RF Studios. Good Time People, Inc. was the name of the production company. And in a weekend we recorded a complete album, in the studio up there on 55th and Broadway. And we had a blast! Had a great time! We thought we were just the best thing since sliced bread. And there were some other famous people in the studio while we were recording all that stuff, so it was a lot of fun! They changed the name of the band that weekend, because Kenny Rogers and the First Edition had a hit with "Condition". So they said, "You don't mind, do you?" And we said, "No. What's the new name?" And they said, "New Mix". And we said, "Okay, that sounds good!" And I don't remember when the artwork was done for that album, because I don't remember being there. But Henry told me that we were there because this famous photographer and artist, who did that illustration on the front and the back of the album, put that thing together and took a bunch of photographs of us during that session up there, but I don't remember that.

DANIEL COSTON: *Whether on the road, or playing in their backyard, a few Charlotte bands found different ways of having fun.*

DONNY FLETCHER: We had some friends from New Jersey that gave us the keys to their frathouse over the summer, and we'd have parties there. The Scotsmen Parties, we used to call them. We'd charge a dollar to get in, no alcohol. Gastonia was still dry, in those days. There was another band called the Botniks, I always loved that name, and they were a couple years younger than us. They'd watched us, and had started a band, so they would open up for us, and then we'd be the big headliner. It all was a big fraternity. We all asked each other about their bands, or whenever you'd seen them play. What kind of stuff do you listen to, what stuff do you like to play?

Coming from Gaston County, we wanted to look as different as you could. If you could get 'em, you got 'em. The big bands in Gastonia were show bands, and like everybody else, we were seeing photos of what was going on. I remember one time playing at the Web, and my hair had gotten a little long. I started looking around, and everyone has torn jeans, t-shirts and long hair, and I thought, "We all look alike." So I cut my hair short, wore Banlons, and loafers. I walked into the Web, and everyone said, "Wow! You've gone straight!"

TIM TATUM: We played at a Battle of the Bands in Lake Norman. There were no towns around. Jimmy Kilgo did a thing up there. Some other band's girlfriends are all there. We came on, and the girls liked us, because we had the uniforms. Each of the bands did a song, and Jimmy Kilgo said, "We're going to bring the Stowaways back on to do another song," since we got the biggest response. And while we were playing, one of the other bands went backstage and dropped the curtain on us.

We finished the song, and went backstage to load up, and the band was back there waiting to fight us. One of them had a switchblade, which kind of scared us, because we didn't know if they all had knives. So we all jumped in our two cars, and gave them the finger! And they decided to chase us. They were throwing beer bottles, trying to push us off the road. We were fish-tailing through stop signs. We finally flagged down a fire truck in a small town, and they took off, after about chasing us for twenty miles.

KEN KNIGHT: One time, we were driving somewhere, and we were tired. So some of us got in the U-haul trailer with the gear, and slept in there. Somebody saw us doing that, and called the police. They pulled us over, and made us get back in the car.

TIM TATUM: We used to shoot bottle rockets out the window while going down the highway. You could get away with a lot more, back then.

DANIEL COSTON: *Another band that was enjoying the life of a Rock & Roll band was the Young Ages, who were getting more high-profile gigs as the year went on.*

JOHN BARKLEY: We could go by Big WAYS anytime after 8pm, and the DJ's would have us on the air. "We've got the Young Ages in the studio." We played a big party for Big WAYS when the movie "Wild In The Streets" opened.

RONNIE PHILLIPS: Another time, we were playing a different movie premiere, and the power went out. I did a 35-minute solo until the power came back on.

JOHN BARKLEY: Girls totally looked at you differently when you were in a band. They wouldn't look at us before, but you put the guitar on, and suddenly it's, "Oh, Johnny."

MIKE RAPER: I've had girls that we went to school with tell us, "I just had the biggest crush on you in school." And I'm like, "Why didn't you do something about it?"

BOB ROBINSON: We toured all across North and South Carolina. We'd play somewhere, get $35, or five bucks a person, get in the bread truck.

MIKE RAPER: We used to put lighter fluid on Ronnie's symbols during "Light My Fire." We also had one of the first strobe lights. Melvin Cohen had found that for us. Nobody knew what that was.

BOB ROBINSON: We got in well with the Greek fraternities. We played for a lot of their fraternities. Those were fun. Some people were here and there about frat parties, but we were all the way there.

On an Easter weekend, we had played for a Key Club in Boone, NC. We played in a clubhouse at the end of a pier, on a lake. The sheriff showed up, and was concerned that we were rocking the clubhouse off of its foundation. We had to turn it down. After playing there, we returned to Charlotte on Sunday. We were riding through the country in our truck. Not having bathed for a couple of days, we were a little rank. Dickie decided to air himself out and stripped off his clothes to hang himself out of the truck. Just as he hung out, we passed by a house where a family was in the front yard, facing the road, posing for a family photo.

JOHN BARKLEY: You should have seen the looks on their faces.

DAVE LONG: One time, we were out with the Young Ages, we got a hotel room, which we rarely did. Johnny, being the country guy that he was, made his hotel room bed in the morning. We were like, "They'll make the bed for you."

JAKE BERGER: By the end of '67, I was back at school and catching a ton of flack from the teachers, and the principal over the style of clothes I was wearing. That attitude would grow as the decade wore on, and the cry of "get a haircut" or some crack about the "hippie clothes" became a common one until the "peace love" started to wear thin, and the normally complacent flower kids started to be a little reluctant to back down. In fact, in one or two more years the jocks and bullies had changed their tune from, "Are you a boy or a girl?" to "Hey man, can you get us some mescaline?" The change in attitude came as the big pop festivals started up, and by the end of the decade Woodstock would jumpstart the homogenization of America's youth culture. The year 1967 ended with a whimper, and gave no hint of the upheaval and riots that would erupt and almost tear the country apart in the following year.

Murder in My Heart for the Judge

DANIEL COSTON: *What gets lost too often to younger fans of the 1960s is that the decade had a lot of bad stuff going on. Civil rights struggles. Pressures and persecution from authorities to keep your hair short, and conform. Or else. Vietnam was everywhere, and going nowhere fast. That was the situation throughout the country. Texas can now talk about their music history all they want, but in the 1960s, persecution from local and state authorities forced nearly all of the state's leading musicians to California, and elsewhere. California also had its own problems, as well, as documented in the 1968 Moby Grape song, "Murder In My Heart For The Judge." The following stories are just a few tales from those in the Charlotte area about their experiences. Their triumphs, their struggles, and incidents that were sadly all too common in those "good old days".*

JAKE BERGER: We were the first generation to have the "miracle technology" of television, and for the first time we got to see the ugly side of America, opening our eyes to the reality as opposed to the myth. A grim reminder! The biggest thing to alter a young person's point of view was the national news, much of which was live and you got the un-varnished truth. Racial tensions were at an all-time high, as people that had been excluded from mainstream American life now were making their frustration known. The news opened the eyes of young whites. Now what had been on the back burner of their minds and not fully been fully aware of was splattered across the seven o'clock news. Now we saw average everyday people caught up in the whirlwind of change. Old ladies, priests, and college kids being swept down the street by fire hoses as they exercised their right to speak out against the injustices of segregation. Cops from another generation with the look of abject hate on their faces as they unleashed police dogs on the protesters. We all saw this early in the decade, but even later in the 60's this lingered.

A local DJ called "Big Al" Earnhardt befriended some of us and would stop by the house on Central Avenue to take a few of us out for a much-needed meal. In the summer of 1969, we went to the House Of Pancakes on East Independence Boulevard. As we waited for service, a sour faced waitress came up and stated, "I have to serve him, but I sure as hell don't have to serve you!" What she was referring to was the young and very black Tony Senior who was with us. After a shocked silence, I looked around to see if anybody witnessed this and what they would have to say about it. What I saw were two Charlotte policemen who snickered in agreement and then threw us out.

The other thing that really sticks in my mind is how violent that time was. During interviews for this book, this is something that repeatedly cropped up, and was a common thread. Early on, before hair and patriotism had become the issue, it was still there. If you were from a different side of town or school, you could be sure somebody would want to fight you. When I was in Junior High, I used to go to hockey games at the old Coliseum, and nearly got into it a couple of times. Later, when hair and the war became an issue, it also became a great excuse to start a fight with someone. I can't explain why this would be, but it started to dissipate in the later 60's, as more and more of the one-time adversaries turned on and came into the fold. There was also a huge polarization over the Vietnam War. Not only was there the standoff between the "peace-nicks" and the All-American kids, but with the parents of these kids, which is where presumably they got their right-wing leanings. This also dissipated as more and more of their sons came home either dead, physically impaired, or just plain mental as anything. By the end of the decade, everyone was tired of the infighting and parents were tired of the alienation from their kids, as well as the parents that never saw their kids again.

ZAN MCLEOD: Jimmy Duckworth and I were standing at the lunch counter at the Eckerd's at Park Road Shopping Center. This guy sees us, and starts yelling about "You lousy people with long hair. I'm going to cut your hair right now," and he pulls out a knife. He was going to cut our hair with force right there. Jimmy yelled, "He's got a knife!" and the whole store to look at the guy, and he froze. We then ran out of the store, and didn't stop until we got to Jimmy's house.

JAKE BERGER: Maybe about 1966, or maybe the next year, just all of a sudden you'd split and it was like, the "button downs" and the people who weren't. It was just before the Hippie thing broke.

BOBBY DONALDSON: Right. Then they "turned on"! That was the word. Once they turned on, it was cool.

JAKE BERGER: Before that, you had to learn to run or fight!

BOBBY DONALDSON: Yeah, it was one or the other! That's just the way it was. I remember one time, I was walking down Selwyn Avenue, right there by Hardee's, and these guys came over and jumped on me just for walking down the street!

JAKE BERGER: Those guys, they turned on about when it became popular for all the high school kids that were graduating. The year before they were not into it, and then suddenly it was, "Hey man, can you get me some?"

BOBBY DONALDSON: Johnny Mattox and I had gone to an Alexander Graham basketball game, and we just happened to have long hair, and it really wasn't any longer than it is right now! And they threw us out of school! I even said, "Mom, I'll get my hair cut", and she said, "No, you won't." And she stuck to her guns. It turned out that she knew the Superintendent of Schools, and he said, "My son's hair is longer than your son's!"

They threw Johnny out of school, and they told him not to come back until he got his hair cut. And so next thing I know, the Superintendent got on the phone and called Mr. Hunt, the principal, and he said, "You need to come over here."

And the first thing he told Mr. Hunt was, "What's the problem with him. What else does he do?" And he said, "Well, nothing, it's just that his hair is causing a disturbance in our school." And he said, " Let me tell you something. My son's hair is longer than his. You let him back in school," and he didn't have to make up any tests, or any days, or anything. And they scolded the principal for throwing me out of school. Matter of fact, Mr. Hunt took me to The Drum Restaurant for lunch, before I went back to school. And then I got my hair cut after I went back to school!

The principal hated me, up until that point. One day, these guys came over from Rock Hill, and they were gonna beat up Johnny Mattox, and they were started to, anyway, and I jumped in there, and it was over with. And from that day on, I was Mr. Hunt's hero! They pushed Mrs. Brown, one of the art teachers, and they knocked her into the bushes and that is when I got involved! I picked her up out of the bushes and then it was kind of on. And after that, with Mr. Hunt, it was like, Ol' Chummy, Ol' Pal.

DEBBY DOBBINS: Garinger High School in 1968 was hardly a friendly place if you had long hair! I remember the first day that Bobby Pace came to school. We were sitting there eating lunch in the cafeteria, and a bunch of the football players who were just thugs jumped him, and threw him down on the floor and tried to cut his hair with scissors. That was his introduction to Garinger.

There was another little guy that year that I remember, Larry Quigley, a little bitty guy, maybe five feet tall. He had long hair, and most of the hippie guys were gone that day, I think that they'd all skipped school and gone to D.C. to see Hendrix, or Cream somewhere.

But a bunch of "Grits," we called them "Grits", or "Banlons". Remember those Banlon shirts that guys wore? Anyway, they were the ones who tormented us for being hippies. Because we wore "love beads" and short skirts, and the guys had the long hair, and wore desert boots and pea coats. But they would come after you. And this one, big, giant ugly Grit guy, and it was me and Karen Loftin, Cindy Locke, Sharon McAuliff and Jennifer Cato were standing around our lockers one morning talking to Larry Quigley and this giant Grit by the name of Leslie Valentine, came up to Larry and starts telling Larry that he's a fag. But anyway, he and a couple of his thug friends come up to Larry, who is like five feet tall, with scissors, and start dragging him into the men's room to cut his hair. We girls threw our books down and ran after them, and just beat the living hell out of them.

I remember that I was on his back, pulling greasy hair, and I grabbed his glasses and threw them on the floor, and Sharon stomped on them! I remember that. And I remember that Cindy was barely five feet tall herself, but she was the first one to throw her books down and take off after them down the hall. And we girls just absolutely beat the crap out of that guy! It ended up going to court, and he got put on probation. It was like big excitement at the school because the hippies had won one, finally!

STEVE STOECKEL: One day, I was in school, and Tim Moore walked in with a new vinyl vest. We were all admiring it, and the teacher said, "Mr. Moore, would you take that vest off? It is hurting my eyes." Tim realized that he was serious, and he said, "No, I'm keeping it on." There was a bit of a standoff, but eventually the teacher did let him keep the vest on. I was impressed, because that took a lot of guts, and Tim was not a big guy.

JAKE BERGER: My friend from Philadelphia, who thought that we'd have plank sidewalks, he was the first person I ever saw that would stand up to that. I remember walking down Central Avenue by Veteran's Park in broad daylight and some car went by and the catcalls came, and Bill went, "F--k you!!!" And the car stopped about half a block away, and Bill picked up a brick and went running down the street and threw it through the back window! They took off. And I was like, "You're gonna get us killed!" No fear! It opened up my eyes a little bit that we didn't have to take that.

DON TETREAULT: You always had to be on guard if there were girls around, because guys always thought that the musicians were out to steal their girlfriends.

JAKE BERGER: Jon and Helen Mullis were living together in the late '60s. They weren't married, but I think they already had one kid. They were proto-hippies, some of the first that lived that way. I think the cops busted them for pot, but they got charged with co-habitation. And the judge ordered them to get married, or go to jail.

TIM TATUM: There was one time that we went to Harris Teeter, and they wouldn't serve us before of our long hair. "I'm sorry boys, but you need to get out of here."

KEN KNIGHT: You'd get whistles. I remember playing to 1500 people in Montgomery, Alabama. We were 45 minutes late, and we showed up and we were getting whistles and catcalls from military guys. We thought, "We're a long way from home."

ROY SKINNER: Myself, Bob [Crawford] and Mike [Wingate] were hitchhiking from Lansing, Michigan to the Detroit airport. As we were walking down the highway, about twenty or thirty cop guys were screaming past us. We were like, "What is going on?" When we got to the airport, we discovered that the riots had started.

ZAN MCLEOD: The fear of Vietnam was terrible. I was in horrible shape for a year, because I got A-1 and a low number. Out of 300, I got 60. There were two things in my favor. The first being that they had plenty of people in the Army that year and they didn't draft quite as many that year, and my birthday was late October. They were also kind of going by birth months, too. I also tried to do a Conscientious Objector thing, at first.

And I was telling them all sorts of things at first. Like I told them that basically I was having LSD flashbacks, for instance. So, they sent me to a shrink, and after I talked to him the last time, they didn't tell me anything. So I was on pins and needles for literally three months, thinking that I was going to be drafted at any time. I couldn't make any plans, and I got a letter one day and I was categorized as 4F! They gave me a 4F! What that means is that not only was I unfit for military service, but I couldn't even work for the government!

But it was bad. A lot of music was influenced by all that. Because of all the protest movements back in those days. The vibe and the music and things were heavily influenced by all that stuff. And the draft was real scary, because it was so random.

ERIC ROBINSON: I was up for the draft, but thankfully I had a high number. A lot of people went to Vietnam, a lot of people went to Canada. A lot of people died during that time.

DENNIS EDWARDS: For the initial period, I was out there for about four months. Then I had to come back because the Draft was after me. I'd gotten my Draft notice, and I had to do something about that. It was either sign up and go to Vietnam and get killed like everybody else, or figure out something to do about it. It was your ass. That was darker than any of these clouds hanging over us.

Here you knew people who had already gone, and they were dead! Most people our age didn't make it. And the ones that came back were messed up. So, I was facing that so I came back. But I was down in Charleston, South Carolina with this girl. I'd gone down there, and we had a hotel room. And there was a TV on this little table in the room and "The Big Picture", the Army TV show, was on. It used to come on every Saturday morning. Back then, there was only a couple of channels on TV, anyway.

The entire 30-minute show was all about LSD. So, I thought, "Okay, let's watch and see what they think about this" and we watched the show and the bottom line about the show was this guy saying, "If you've taken LSD, you can be going along three months later or even a year from then, and just get high all over again! Even if you only take it one time." So I thought to myself, "If they believe that, then maybe I've got an angle."

So, I put that off for a little while and was just piddling around, and then I got the notice that I had to go down, over there on Pecan Avenue. I had to go down for my physical, and I only had like a week before I had to go report for my physical. So, I got that letter and I immediately called the Mental Health Clinic. And I said, "I need to speak to a doctor right now." And the nurse said," He's busy, what can I help you with?" And I said, "I've taken some LSD and I need to talk to somebody about the effects." And boom! The doctor got on the phone, "Can you come down here?" So I go down there and it's after hours, it's after 5pm, and I get in there and there's not only that doctor, there's five or six of them all around the table.

I was the first person they had ever seen that came in and admitted that they'd taken LSD. And they said, "What is the problem?" And I said, "Well, I'm just kinda high. All the time. No matter what I do." And boy, did they buy it! Hook, line and sinker. They had me going down there every day talkin' to 'em and doing tests. And I just kind of acted like I had all the time in the world.

Finally, it got to be crunch time, and I asked the doctor to write me a letter. And he wrote me this great letter. Because back then, you didn't know if a doctor was for the war or against the war, I didn't know. But he wrote me this letter. And I go down for the physical, and you were just a piece of meat back then, they strip you down. You don't have any rights, and I don't know how many times they said to me, "You say anything, and you are on the bus to Ft. Bragg right now! And you'll be in Vietnam in 48 hours."

So, I waited, and finally, on the questionaire I wrote under the question, "Are you under treatment for any condition?" that I was, "Under treatment for extensive use of LSD." And I'm walking around with this piece of paper, naked, and I noticed that this guy sees that part of the questionnaire. And he says to me, "Are you taking drugs right now?" And I said, "No man, I don't have to." That's all I said.

And he sent me over to the hearing test. So in the hearing test, they put you in this big chamber and about 20 guys at a time go in and put these headphones on, and they give you this beeper. And they tell you, "When you hear a sound, press the beeper, and when you don't hear a sound, just let it go." And I'm sitting in there, and I don't hear anything, so I don't press the beeper. And this guy comes in and screams at me that I'm trying to mess with the army. I said, "I didn't hear anything." It turned out that the headphones were broken. So we went through the test again, and I went through it, but I got the deferment to get out.

After that, I went back to California for about 8 or 9 years. As soon as I got out of the Army thing, I had to leave town or I was going to go to jail because we were doing drugs, and we were the only hippie kids around.

SHORTY NEHRENBERG: The police chief of Charlotte got us downtown one day and sat us down in a circle and said, "Everyone of y'all is either gonna leave Charlotte or go to jail, and we don't care which. We are gonna get you, and it's just a matter of time."

I moved to California for two reasons, and one was to not get arrested, which I knew was imminent if I'd stayed around, it was just going to happen. And two, was not to get killed by some redneck on the street.

ROB THORNE: Around here in the southeast, guys that I knew, even myself, when we started letting our hair grow long and we became "hippie-fied". It got pretty weird. People would say things to you in the streets. And even in some of the clubs, some of the short-haired rednecky guys took offense to it. I remember one time at the Cellar, some guy was gonna beat me up because I had long hair and a beard. And I was in the band! And I thought, "Wait a minute, I'm immune to this kind of stuff. What are you talkin' about? I'm with the band." And he said, "So what? I'm still gonna beat your ass!" But he never did. I think a bouncer threw him out.

But it was only because I looked different from the way he did. And that what was so intimidating to these people. All of a sudden, a bunch of weird looking people, looking "too different" just upset their comfort zones. A lot of bands had that trouble. Especially young kids.

I was at Ft. Bragg in 1969, and a lot of guys were just coming back from Vietnam. The company that I was in was a support group, and a lot of these "return-ees" were filtered back into companies that were a part of my support brigade, and all it was, was a "holding pen" for these guys until they were mustered out. Some of these guys maybe had two weeks left in the Service, some might have had six months left in after their rotation out of Vietnam, and these were mostly ground troops, "grunts", and of fairly low rank.

But it was not uncommon for a group of people to come in on a Monday or a Tuesday, and over the weekend prior to that had been in an intense fire fight over there in

Vietnam! And then, all of a sudden their time was up on Sunday, and by Monday or Tuesday they were back in the United States at Ft. Bragg, and they were expected to "behave like soldiers." And do what they were "supposed to do" in a non-combatant situation. Well, they couldn't handle this! Especially the ones who had been in heavy combat often, and most of them were. Especially the Infantry Troops. And, God, it was unbelievable! I became very anti-war at that time. During the last part of that year that I was in down there, because I saw all of that shit coming back and the way they were treated.

SHORTY NEHRENBERG: Everywhere you went at night, they literally wanted to kill you. It was, "Let's stop the car and get a tire iron out of the trunk and chase you through the woods and kill you!" We were literally told to leave places just because of the way we looked. In other words, you'd walk into the restaurant and sit down, and they'd say, "Get out!" You walk into a pool hall and they say, "Leave!" And you'd ask why and they'd say, "Because we don't like you."

I'll never forget, I went to the beach with my girlfriend and we were swimming and got caught in a riptide and I thought we were going to die. We finally got out of the ocean, got to the shore and collapsed. We were dead tired. So we just wanted to go home. We get in the car and start driving and decided to stop at the first place we could find to get something to eat and kind of regroup. And we get to some little city in South Carolina, and just as soon as we hit the city limits I saw the cop, I saw him pull out behind us.

So we get to a little diner and just as soon as the food comes, the big old fat sheriff comes in, sits down in front of us and starts harassing the hell out of us. So we realized that if we didn't get out of there, something bad was gonna happen. I mean we had to leave, or he was gonna find something to arrest us for. And that is what it was like for us around here. Every day. So, you kind of quickly knew who your friends were and who weren't, it was kind of obvious. And you'd quickly gravitate to people who could help you out when you got into these kinds of situations, because a lot of times, it was serious. Things could go very wrong very quickly. Your friends are dying in Vietnam and your friends are dying in the street. You could go to a store to just get an ice cream cone and find yourself in big trouble.

So you lived on that kind of edge all the time. Your parents didn't really understand what you were going through, nobody did. We could identify with the Black cause, because we felt the same way! Everywhere we'd go, people were trying to kill us.

I used to go out driving, and the police would pull me over for having long hair, and find something to cite me for. Eventually, the tickets piled up, and I had to go to traffic court. I was there in a suit, with my parents.

I walked in, and the judge started talking aloud about how you can't tell the girls from the boys. He never looked at me, but after the sixth time he said that, I started to get annoyed. So I said, "You must have some interesting dates." And the judge said, "$200 fine, two weeks in jail," and they started to haul me away before he was even finished.

I couldn't believe it. I'd look at my fellow inmate and say, "What are you in for?" and he'd say, "I murdered my wife, what are you in for?" "Traffic ticket". It was insane! I'm seventeen years old and sitting in jail for two weeks with hardened criminals and the dregs of society just because some judge didn't like the length of my hair!

County jail was bad. I was attacked, and someone had to come save me. I saw two guys get killed. My bunk got set on fire one night. By the third day, the sheriff called me to his office, and said, "If you'll cut your hair, you can go free." At this point, I was in shock from what I'd gone through, but I was hardened. I said, "No thanks," and walked back to my cell. After a few days of that, the inmates gave me some respect, and left me alone.

Later, I was a senior at South Meck, and they would never measure me for my cap and gown. They eventually told me, "You will not walk across that stage with that long hair." I was almost done with the year, and I wanted to go to California. I told the teacher that I needed to have an operation done, and could I take the last test early? She said yes, and I got a B+, which meant I had the required English to graduate.

Somebody told on me, and the principal called me and my father into the office, and ripped up my last test in front of us. I ended up taking summer school at Myers Park, and getting my diploma there. Yes, I had not told the truth, but the principal was going to find a way to keep me off of that stage. The principal, the police, all these people that these longhairs were just a few troublemakers, and if they went away, then the problem would go away.

DENNIS EDWARDS: We had encounter after encounter with people after you, trying to cut your hair. So I go off to California and stay for about eight years, and come back here to visit and everyone's got hair down to their ass! Including the rednecks who were trying to kill us back then!

SHORTY NEHRENBERG: It was the music that united everybody. You'd hear a song and you knew that you and your buddies all over the country were into that same thing. That's why it was so important, because it was all you had. Years later, you saw the world had completely changed. People whom I knew who'd spent four or five years in Vietnam had changed, and the very things that I'd been trying to promote, they weren't so against anymore. I got that a lot, after that. Guys that hated me in high school had gone through Vietnam. "I'm sorry I tried to kill you." But so much had been lost, it was hard to feel like we had won.

On the Air

JAKE BERGER: Another major influence in my life was the TV, or the pipeline to "what was happening" in the world of the young. Programs like "Hullabaloo", "Where The Action Is", and "The Lloyd Thaxton Show" were staples, and every Wednesday night after "Combat!" at 8:00 p.m. came "Shindig!" "Shindig" was an American idea with an English host, what would almost 20 years later be re-named a VJ. All the acts performed live, and you got the best of the best. The Rolling Stones, at their peak. The Beatles. The Beau Brummels, a new group with an outrageously brash sound. The Kinks, the Zombies, and scads more. Even the Everly Brothers were the "house band" for a while, before handing that chore over to the "Shin-dogs".

Then there was "Hullabaloo", with the artists of the day miming their current single. Their first house band, the Gauchos, was the first band I ever saw that sported two drummers. The second house band, the Hullabaloos, consisted of such luminaries as Glen Campbell and Leon Russell. And of course, the afternoon programs. "Lloyd Thaxton", and "Where The Action Is", designed to keep the young off the streets and away from school work. I watched like a recently saved convert. The Thaxton show was a more typical format much like our own local Saturday afternoon youth oriented show, "Kilgo's Canteen". Kids dancing to the hits, and a band performing as a highlight. Kilgo's was live, and Thaxton was lip-synced. I think at this point I saw Bobby Donaldson with the Greystones doing the Beatles song, "This Boy", on Kilgo's Canteen. In an age where MTV has been commonplace for 30 years it seems insignificant, but then it was a first, and an important format, without which, there would be no MTV.

PAT WALTERS: You'd hear it on the radio. Maybe one song, then you'd get the album, and of course, all your friends would have something that you didn't have, and you'd devour that. And then the magazines that were out, magazines like "The Hit Parader" had interviews with The Yardbirds. So all of a sudden, there's a picture with Jimmy Page. We knew who Jimmy Page was before there was a Led Zeppelin. We'd read all about him, it was a good way to keep informed. That was before "Rolling Stone".

I guess that even though we grew up in Charlotte, and we weren't able to see a lot of those bands live like you could in some parts of the country then, but we got to see quite a few, and there was always TV. So, yeah, the Yardbirds were on "Shindig" maybe a couple of times, and certainly the early British Invasion bands were all over TV.

DANIEL COSTON: *By the mid 1960s, the TV networks were airing several shows that showcased the new bands and sounds. At the same time, numerous local TV dance shows were also popping up across the country. Many had local students come in to talk about, and dance to the new records of the day. Others featured local, or regional bands. In Charlotte, the longest running teen music show had originally begun as a radio show.*

JIMMY KILGO: "Kilgo's Canteen" signed on in April of 1957. We had only room to do everything. News, weather, the Canteen, so we had a lot of logistics to work out. Having done the radio show, we had a better sense of logistics, and what we could do.

The radio show started in the Hawthorne Recreation Center. I talked to them and told them what I wanted to do. To have a place where the kids could come after school, and spent an hour, talk and dance. The radio show was also called "Kilgo's Canteen", and started around 1954, or 1955. I then decided that I needed some TV experience. At the time, there was only one TV station in Charlotte, which was WBT. WSOC had just been granted a license. I went to work at WSKS in Winston-Salem for about a year, and then came back to audition to be one of the original newscasters for WSOC. I moved back to town a week before we signed on, in April of 1957.

We had no problems. The format that we set up for the radio show, turned out to be great for TV. It was a great show for the TV station, and I'm saying that without any conceit, or narcissistic attitude. I required the boys to wear suit coat and ties, and the girls to wear their school clothes, which was not conducive to making trouble.

Three or more months after the show started, I went to management. This was during the age of segregation, and I told them, "We're missing something." About 25 percent of our population at that time was black, and you had West Charlotte High School. I said, "I think we should reserve one Saturday a month for our black students." They were all in agreement with me, and that turned out to be very good. At the beginning, I got all kinds of threats over the phone. All this crap, which I expected, and ignored. Within three months, the calls changed to, "I really like it when you have those black students on. They really can dance." So a whole flip-flop took place.

We would hold auditions every three months, and have all the people that were interested in playing in a combo come on in. We'd line up the talent for the next three months, and start all over again. We were lucky enough to have established groups like the Catalinas come on the program, and any traveling artists that were in the area. Johnny Tillotson, Gene Pitney.

DANIEL COSTON: *Gill Vanderlip's band the Screws were one of many bands that auditioned for "Kilgo's Canteen".*

GILL VANDERLIP: Kilgo's was a big deal. The word just got out that if you wanted to be on "Kilgo's Canteen", you had to audition. So I had a band. And my mom packed us all up in her truck and we went. There were a lot of bands, and good bands! And we were just in Junior High School. We were still wet behind the ears! We didn't know, we just played parties at school.

I was 15 when I was on "Kilgo's Canteen". That was 1967. For the audition we played, "Wipe Out" And then the guy said, "I want to hear you sing something", and then we did, "Gloria". And what got us the gig, is when we did "Gloria" we stopped the song, and Stan and Rich would hit the kick. And then we'd start again, like a reprise. And they loved that! Because they thought the song was over, and we'd start it again!

collection of Gill Vanderlip

Loose Screws on "Kilgo's Canteen," 1967.

The first time on the show we played, "We Gotta Get Out Of This Place" by The Animals. I took the bass and changed a couple of notes and made it a guitar part. The bass would never cut through your little TV's. So we took the bass part and we took a guitar and cut the treble off, and when you hit the guitar note from the E-string, it would cut through the TV! So we did, "We Gotta Get Out Of This Place" by changing it around, and we did "Good Lovin'" by The Rascals.

That was in black and white. And then, after the show had started airing in color, we came back and we did, "Gloria." I played bass on that! I took my Silvertone guitar and de-tuned E down to D, because all the treble cut through the little TV's. Because I noticed a lot of bands, you could never hear the bass guitar! You could never hear the bass! Never! It was just always gone! And then we did, "What I'd Say" by Ray Charles. It was a lot of fun!

DANIEL COSTON: *What was the response like from your classmates?*

GILL VANDERLIP: They liked us, but they thought we were funny because we were "mocking" The Beatles with Beatle haircuts, and guitars and stuff. You know, it was fine, whatever, but we really didn't get that much response. The musicians will give you the response! Or your family. But the average kid in school didn't give us much response.

ROB THORNE: The Catalinas used to go on the show and dance, and show the new dance moves.

RUSSELL HODGE: I was with a group called the Excels. We backed up a guy that went by the name of "West Side James Brown". Back then, you didn't have the interest, media coverage and fan magazines that you do now. So to see yourself on television was pretty usual. There also weren't many television sets back then.

ZAN MCLEOD: Most of the local bands played on there. The Die Hards played on there. I went there with them to the studio when they played. They did a lot of the classic covers at that time, tunes like, "Time Won't Let Me". They did that era right in there, right after The Beatles were hot. Sort of post-Mersey beat, but pre-psychedelic. "Hey Joe", or the Blues Magoos. Radio tunes, almost psychedelic. Mike Falkenberry was the lead guitar player, and he was good. He might have been the best one around, really, and he is the guy who taught me a lot of stuff.

PAT WALTERS: So we showed up for Kilgo's, and Phil Lowe didn't bring his drums. He might have had to cut something out of some poster-board to beat on, or that's a bass drum and beat on the "air drums"! And so we were "green screened" with primitive psychedelic effects on TV. And that was that experience.

TOM POPE: One time, we were on "Kilgo's Canteen", and we were playing "Johnny B. Goode". I hit that lead [guitar solo], and they zoomed in on my guitar. I thought, "This is great! I'm on TV!" There was also a show on channel 36, what WCNC is now. Their studios were out on Hood Road. They had a show like "Kilgo's Canteen". I think it was called "36 Bandstand". We were on that show twice, and they re-ran that episode around six times.

DANIEL COSTON: *At the same time, a number of syndicated programs were coming through WBTV, which had one of the strongest TV signals in the Southeast US. This included Arthur Smith's syndicated TV show, and the popular "Village Square" series.*

ZAN MCLEOD: WBTV was the center of music! It really was.

DANIEL COSTON: *"The Village Square" had begun in Myrtle Beach in 1964. The show featured their house band, the Villagers, playing the top songs of the day. The show was syndicated in over 50 cities, and made regional stars out of guitarist Wayne West, and singer Jeanne Lavoie. By 1966, the show was taping at WBTV studios, which gave some Charlotte bands the chance to appear on the show as special guests. This included the Catalinas, the 18th Edition (before they changed their name to the New Mix), and the Paragons.*

PAT WALTERS: I don't recall much about doing "Village Square". Just being in a big studio with sets and bunch of friendly people. We were kids and it was tremendous fun. We were gonna be on TV! I recall Chatty Hattie, a DJ with WGIV radio, was very nice to me. She asked me how I liked being in show business. I'd never thought about show business before that, just being in a band. They would tape a lot of segments for different shows and edit them together later. I do remember that the Catalinas, with Rob Thorne on drums, were there taping. I didn't know him at that time. They were grown men!

DANNY HUNTLEY: The Villagers became friends through Johnny Pace, I believe, and they use to be the star attraction at Myrtle Beach when they had the big beach dance hall on the second level of The Pavilion. We traveled some with The Villagers as guests, and when they got their show on WBTV, "The Village Square", a once-a-weekend show, they asked us to appear.

We played on WTVI for a program to teach kids about rock music. It was called, "Granny Goes Grooving". This was a program sponsored by the Charlotte Mecklenburg School system and played in schools. This was a series, but how many, I do not remember. We also played several times on a very popular local program on WSOC called "Kilgo's Canteen" and it was patterned after American Bandstand. But teenagers were invited to come on and dance to popular songs of the time, with Jimmy Kilgo as the MC.

DANIEL COSTON: *While TV was continuing those that wanted to see what their favorite bands looked like, radio was still king across the country. If your record was to be discovered and sold, you had to get airplay.*

LARRY SPRINKLE: If we played it, it was bought. If Big WAYS played it, it was bought. That's how people found the music. There were a lot of big name DJs in town during the '60s. Jack Gail at Big WAYS. He was also the program director. If Jack picked a record and played it, it sold. He was as important as the record. You had Long John Silver, Dickie Doo, Melvin The Grocery Boy, Mike Green. Over at WIST, you had Dave Bell and George Brown. AT WGIV you had Rocking Ray Gooding, Chatty Hattie Leeper, Genial Gene Potts, Brother Ross The Boss. And Ray Gooding, and Chatty Hattie Leeper at WGIV.

STEVE STOECKEL: You found songs through the radio. WIST, WNYS. You'd hear them on the radio, and search out these records. They might have only one song worth a damn, but the radio stations ruled, entirely.

BOBBY DONALDSON: Living around here, we were fortunate enough to have WGIV and some of the other black radio stations. It's like, in the mornings, when I was on my way to A.G. or to Myers Park. That was where my radio was tuned to in my little '62 Corvair! And the bands that I played with, those were the songs that we wanted to play, so it came naturally. I guess it's just what I came up with.

DANIEL COSTON: *Several local radio stations in Charlotte sponsored Battle Of The Bands contests, or had local musicians play live on the air.*

BOBBY DONALDSON: I was with a band that played the WIST mezzanine at Belk's department store. It was Barbara Harding and Don Cross, and we actually played live on the radio! I remember our drummer didn't have his bass drum tied down, so he laid the tom-tom part of the bass drum on the Wurlitzer piano. The floor of the mezzanine at Belk's was quite slick, and it was live on the radio when the drums slid up and the whole drum set fell over! Live on the air! We were playing that song, "Oh where, oh where can my baby be?" "Last Date", J. Frank Wilson and the Cavaliers, when that drum set fell over! I can't remember ten minutes ago, but I can remember that, 50 years ago!

BOB ROBINSON: J.W. Morgan was the midnight DJ at WAYS. The Young Ages would on numerous occasions visit him during his shows. At the time, psychedelic music was just coming around to the Charlotte market. Long John Silver was the prime-time DJ. WAYS allowed him, and only him, to play "Purple Haze", Light My Fire" and "Sunshine Of Your Love" (Long John announced it as "Sunshine Of Your Smile, by the Creek") during his program. He kept the 45's locked on a small steel box, so that no one else could play them. We found the box one night and tried to open it, because J.W. was determined that he should be allowed to air them. We never succeeded. It was a pretty hefty little box.

DANIEL COSTON: *Every DJ in Charlotte has a story as to how they came to town. For Larry Sprinkle, his journey to the Charlotte airwaves took many detours.*

LARRY SPRINKLE: I came to Charlotte at WIST, in 1969. I was here from September of 1969, to January of 1970, and then I went to Memphis for three years. It was known as the Barringer Hotel, and then it was known as the Cavalier Inn. The station was in one of the top floors. It was a critical time for the country, a time of a lot of turmoil. The war was not popular, at all. It was also a big time of transition for music, and rock music, especially. Some of the longtime beach music bands were switching over to rock music, or having more of an edgier rock sound, to attract that crowd.

I was born in North Carolina, but lived all over. My father was an engineer, so we lived all over. I lived in Winston-Salem the longest, about six years. I also used to go through Charlotte Airport, and used to go see a lot of shows at Park Center.

I became obsessed with music, and radio when I was five. I started on the air at Forest City, NC when I was 14. It was a small radio station. If you could breathe, they'd hire you to work there. My voice was still changing, but I was aggressive, and enthusiastic, and they give me a two-hour show every day after school. They played Top 40, which was everything from Barbara Streisand, to the Rolling Stones, to the Temptations and Conway Twitty.

On the weekends, they would specialize in different types of music. I would be on the air all day on Saturday. I had a country music show, a blues show, a jazz show, an easy listening show, a gospel music show on Sunday, and Top 40 during the afternoon. My program director said, "If you're going to work for me, you're going to learn this music, and you're going to appreciate it. And you'll thank me for it." And he was right.

When I was 15, there was a big furniture plant that opened up in Forest City. The manager came from Youngstown, Ohio, and he had a son who was my age. The son and I became friends, and some point, he said, "Hey Larry, my brother was two TV shows in New York City, and they're kind of like American Bandstand. He's coming to see me, would you like to talk to him? His name is Clay Cole." Clay came, and I interviewed him on the radio, and Clay said, "If you ever come to New York City, you need to be on my show."

Two months later, my journalism class went on a field trip to Columbia University. I called him, and he said, "You're going to be on the show." It was set up like a cafe style. The guests that day were Tony Bennett, the Manhattans, and the Rolling Stones. After the show, Clay said, "I want you to meet these guys." Here I am, a nerdy 14 year-old kid. Flat-top haircut. Clay takes me into their room, and introduces me, and they're thinking, "Who the hell is this kid?" They didn't even talk to me. Finally, Keith Richards said, "Clay, where's the fooking birds?" I couldn't stand the Stones for years after that, because of that, but I finally became a fan, again.

When I was 16, we moved to Ethiopia, in East Africa. I'm a teenager in the United States, I have my own radio show, and all of a sudden, my dad says, "We're moving to East Africa." I thought it was the end of the world. I thought I would never be in radio again.

We moved to Addis Ababa, which is a major city. And in that city, there was the Ministry Of Information, which was Radio Ethiopia. They had dozens of stations, on dozens of frequencies. I started listening to the English language portion. The first thing I did was go down and apply for a job, and they almost laughed at me. "How old are you? We can't hire you." Within two months, I got a call, and they desperately needed someone to do a show. So I started working there.

I had friends of mine send me tapes of the latest hits in the United States. You couldn't finds that music anywhere in the country, and I would get the tapes a week later, and put them on the air. It was shortwave, and AM. Imagine a 100,000 watt AM station, and a shortwave band. It blasted all over the Middle East. I got mail from all over the Middle East, and into Greece.

DANIEL COSTON: *By 1969, Sprinkle was back in North Carolina. An infamous on-air accident would soon bring him to Charlotte.*

LARRY SPRINKLE: The Phantasmagoria was out in the middle of nowhere, and it was a Rock & Roll club. It was a "hippy club." Totally underground. At night, for two hours, WIST would do a live show out there, with a DJ broadcasting live from the Phantasmagoria. One night, two DJs are out there, on the air, and there's a guy back at the station who is running the board. He's thinking, "These guys are out there on the air, I'll go take a break." He went to the hamburger joint across the street.

All of the sudden, back at the club, the DJ's VU meters go dead. "What's going on?" They don't know it, but their mics are still live, and there's no one back at the station. "I guess we're off the air," and they proceed to talk about controversial things about using drugs, people selling drugs, some profanity. This goes on for 40 minutes on the air, live. By then, the guy running the board goes back to the station, and the phones are just lighting up. He hears what's going on, and says, "Oh my God!" and cuts off the feed. He calls out to the club, and says, "Hey, what are you guys doing? You've been on the air," and the phone went dead. One of the guys left town that night, another got fired the next day.

I was hired to take the place of one of those DJs, but the station didn't tell me about what had happened. At that point, I was at a programmed country music station in Cherryville, NC at the time, and the station called and said, "Hey, we got your tape. Can you come to work with us?" The first night I was on the air, I got all these calls. "You nasty lowlife hippy", and all these horrible things, thinking that I was that other DJ. That went on for weeks, and weeks. That incident was legendary in radio circles, for years. Not just here, but in other cities.

DANIEL COSTON: *Despite the incident, WIST continued their remote broadcasts from Phantsamagoria, with Sprinkle's assistance. What Sprinkle did not take part in was the ongoing pushing of the radio envelope.*

LARRY SPRINKLE: WIST's competition was Big WAYS, which was Top 40. WIST promoted themselves as having a harder edge. A lot of underground music. Sometimes, you were tempted to push the edge. I was afraid to push that envelope. I felt I was lucky to have a job there. The closest I got was playing the new Temptations record. One Sunday morning, one of the WIST DJs decided to push the envelope. He figured, "Who's listening on a Sunday morning?" He played Steppenwolf's album all the way through. It opens with "The Pusher". In the song, John Kay yells, "God Damn the Pusher Man!" Everybody went crazy. It got press for weeks. The media, and the newspapers talked about the station playing this controversial song. The station was always getting attention for the music they played, and what the DJs did on and off air.

From the time that I was a kid, I wanted to be on the air. I wanted to meet all of these musicians, and be a part of the music. Looking back, it was an exciting time for music, and it was an exciting time for radio.

CHAPTER ELEVEN
Eastern N.C. Scene

DANIEL COSTON: *After Pat Walters left the Paragons in early 1968, he visited Chapel Hill to do some exploring, and plot his next move.*

PAT WALTERS: What was the Chapel Hill scene like? Hippies! My older siblings lived up there, so I went up there to hang out for the summer. To get away from the bad scene in Charlotte. And when I got back, we started putting GBU together.

DANIEL COSTON: *In the early 1960s, Chapel Hill was much like the rest of the state. Bands like the Embers and the Catalinas were popular at dances. One early frat-rock band that forged their own trail was Doug Clark and the Hot Nuts. Formed in 1960, Clark made his name with R&B, Rock & Roll, and novelty songs that were often of a sexual nature. Often performing in various states of undress, the Hot Nuts became the band that the fraternities loved to hire for their parties, even if they didn't tell their college advisor, or their parents. Clark also began pressing his own albums on the Gross Records label in 1961, and sold the records at their shows. The band's first album, Nuts To You, featured Clark flipping the middle finger to an audience member. The band went on release nine albums during the 1960s.*

BOB HINKLE: Doug Clark and the Hot Nuts were a little more on the raunchy side, which was appealing to someone of my age, at the time.

DANIEL COSTON: *By 1963, the folk revival was in full swing in Chapel Hill, opening the door for a number of new acts to spring up.*

BOB HINKLE: In 1964, I met up with a guy from North Wilkesboro. His name was Bill Swafford, who later became Oliver. Between Bill, myself and Andy Shepherd, who was from Goldsboro, we formed a group called the Townhouse Three. There was a great coffeehouse in Durham that we played a lot. We also played a lot of places. We changed our name to the Virginians, I can't remember why. We got a record contract. We had a single deal with Mercury, and then with Epic. We had an album deal with Dynavoice, which was a Decca subsidiary owned by Bob Crewe.

When we got to Dynovoice, we changed our name to the Good Earth. We toured across the country. We did a lot of touring with Mitch Ryder. We'd do our show, and then we'd change clothes and sing backup for Mitch. We also sang on his records. If you hear the low harmony, that's me.

My schedule as a student was based on what I thought the professor's feelings would be if I didn't show up a fair amount of the time. I did graduate, but I don't know how. We did have one hit on WKIX, a song on Epic Records called "Long Walk Back To Paradise". I did also play with a fun party band in Chapel Hill called the Magucci Bowling Team.

The Virginians got big enough that the University took note of us. They booked us to open for Doc and Merle Watson at the student center. After the show, someone said, "Can you guys come over and say hello?" The school is trying to recruit for the basketball team." So we went over. Dean Smith was there, and we met Charlie Scott, who went on to be a star at UNC, and later in the NBA. So the school used us to help with recruiting.

DANIEL COSTON: *In 1964, Isaac Taylor was chosen to become Dean of the UNC School Of Medicine. His five children would all figure in the Chapel Hill music scene throughout the 1960s. In 1963, eldest son Alex Taylor formed the Corsayors, which also featured Vic Lipscomb, Steve Oakley, Cam Schinan, and Buck Williams. The band developed a following by playing frat parties, after football games, and other places near the UNC campus.*

By 1964, Alex had welcomed his younger brother James into the band. James Taylor would only play with the group for several months, but would contribute to the band's recordings, as well as the only single that the band released during that time. The A-side of that single, "Change Your Ways," was written by Alex Taylor, and was released as a single by the JCP label that same year. Despite's James' return to Milton Academy in Massachusetts in 1965, the Corsayors (who would later go by the Fabulous Corsairs) remained popular in Chapel Hill for some time.

LIVINGSTON TAYLOR: My parents had a lot of showtunes-type stuff around. Plays like Kismet, My Fair Lady, Carousel, Oklahoma. My earliest memories are some of those songs. At the same time, our oldest brother Alex was bringing home lots of music. Lots of R&B, Ike & Tina Turner, Elvis Presley, Bobby "Blue" Bland, the Swan Silvertones. We were also listening to Woody Guthrie, Pete Seeger. So there was a fairly musical group around our house.

HUGH TAYLOR: I remember Alex coming home with Meet The Beatles. It seemed like he got one of the first copies of the album in Chapel Hill. I remembered that we all listened to the harmonies, and we said, "We can do that", and we all started singing the harmonies together.

The bands that I was in played a lot of frat parties when I was really young, when I was 12, and 13 years old. The frat houses, or the sororities had an entertainment budget, and maybe twice a year they'd dole it out for the bigger R&B names, like the Platters. But by the middle of the week, they would still be drinking beer, and they would get tired of the jukebox, so they'd often hire us to come in and play on weeknights. I remember telling my parents that I was practicing out at someone's else, when in fact we were playing at ten bucks apiece out at some frathouse.

We had a couple of different bands. Some of the names, I don't even remember. It was a lot of the same players, and some of them went in and out of the groups. The Crescendos was one that I was with. That was a fairly long-lived one. There was another one called the Bedpost Reunion. That was a tongue-in-cheek name.

We played frat row frequently, and lots of youth halls under churches. We also played at least once in a memorably named coffeehouse type club at Duke called The Celestial Omnibus. We also played a few times to black audiences at places like the Aloha Club, in Carrboro.

LIVINGSTON TAYLOR: I was definitely in the folk music direction. When I was 13, I sang with a woman named Kim Page, and another fellow named Paul Collins, and we had a folk trio. That lasted for about a year.

HUGH TAYLOR: The first time I was really knocked out by one of my family members was when I saw my sister Kate sing at a show. Paul Collins backed her up on guitar, and she sang "Boys" by the Shirelles. And I was like, "Wow! She's a really great singer."

DANIEL COSTON: *Folk, frat-rock and beach music would continue to stay popular in Chapel Hill for much of the decade. Slowly, a few more Rock & Roll-oriented acts began to emerge, such as the Nomads, Vogues, Shackles, and others. The Sands Of Time, which featured Mel Jones, Dickie Andrews, Skip Via, Biff Breem, Don Fuller and Don Sparrow, enjoyed a sizable following in the Chapel Hill area. Another group during the late 1960s was the Minority, led by John Hostetler, who was from Charlotte. Hostetler would later return to Charlotte to sing with August, as well as a later version of the Paragons.*

There was one group from Chapel Hill that did break away from the pack. The Nova Local was formed in 1965 by singer Randy Winburn, guitarist Phil Lambeth, bassist Jim Opton and drummer Bill Levasseur. The band had their sights on more than just the

Triangle area, leading them to the release of their sole album, Nova 1, on Decca Records in 1967.

PHIL LAMBETH: I belonged to the music fraternity at UNC, and during my sophomore year a group of us got together to form a combo. There was another student group called The Shadows that played mostly the music of the British Invasion, and they became wildly popular almost immediately. However, it turned out that the bass player and the lead guitar player had to leave for some reason at the end of the school year and the group then disbanded. The bass player in our group, enterprising fellow that he was, grabbed me by the arm when he heard the news, and went to the two remaining and now-unemployed members of the Shadows with the suggestion that we were just the guys to take the place of the departed ones. We got together one day for a session in the basement of their fraternity house to check out our sound, and we seemed to click from the very beginning. And so were The Shadows reborn during my junior year of college, with me playing lead guitar (and later the electric organ, as well).

We did quite well and kept the group together for our senior year, but in keeping with the mod flavor of the times we changed our name to The Luved Ones. Looking back, I don't know how I ever found the time to go to class and do my basic assignments, let alone graduate, because it seemed like we were playing at frat parties every weekend and rehearsing several times during the week.

The music fraternity I belonged to brought Chad & Jeremy to Chapel Hill for a campus concert that fall, and it didn't take too much string-pulling to arrange for The Luved Ones to open their show. Chad & Jeremy's agent liked us so much that he signed us up on the spot for a recording contract. Over the Christmas holidays we were off to New York to record some demos. Decca Records must have liked what they heard, because they asked us back to cut a full-blown album under a new name: The Nova Local (a take-off, I suppose, on Nova Express, a camp novel by William Burroughs). A test market single was released that spring for the Chapel Hill market. The A side was "If You Only Had The Time," and I believe it got up to #15 or so on the local radio station.

I spent the summer following graduation bedding down at the bass player's family home near New Haven, and we would commute back and forth to New York City for studio session time, and the various gigs that the Decca agent was able to get for us. That was one of the most memorable and frenetic summers of my life. I remember one time we showed up at Columbia Studios for a recording session right when The Happenings were packing up from doing a Great Shakes commercial. We rubbed elbows with some mighty fine musicians. Charlie Fox, who wrote the music for Happy Days and other television hit shows, did some string arrangments for our pieces. Our album was also the first LP to be recorded using the Dolby NR system.

With the summer drawing to a close, I had a decision to make. I had been accepted to law school for the fall term at UNC. So should I roll the dice and hope that we would strike it rich in the world of rock music, or should I say thanks for the memories and go on back to school? I opted for the latter, and I've never regretted my decision. As it turned out, the guys replaced me with a better lead guitarist [Joe Mendyk], and a better organ player [Cam Schinhan], although I've enjoyed being able to boast that it took two warm bodies to fill my shoes. But they fizzled out, and broke up less than a year later.

DANIEL COSTON: *The Triangle area of North Carolina (Chapel Hill, Raleigh, and Durham) had than their fair share of bands during the 1960s. Some of these bands received airplay on Raleigh's WKIX radio station, while others in to the TV show "Teenage Frolics", which ran on WRAL channel 5, and was hosted by J. D. Lewis.*

The Si-Dells, from Durham, released one single in 1968 on the East Coast Sound label. Si-Dells founder Hubert Deans was also in a later version of the Bondsmen. Another Durham band, the Dukes made an appearance on the nationally televised "Happening '69," hosted by Mark Lindsay, and Paul Revere & The Raiders.

The Horde was formed in 1966 by a group of students at Duke University. Playing a mix of originals and covers, the quintet quickly veered towards a more psychedelic sound. After recording a then-unreleased EP in Greensboro in 1967, the band recorded a full-length album that same year, and printed only a handful of copies. The band's entire output was reissued by the German label Break-A-Way Records in 2013.

The Bondsmen may well have been Durham's most popular band. The band won several Battle Of The Bands competitions, and released two singles. Their drummer was a young Philip Pearson, who has since gone on to record and tour internationally as Phil Lee.

PHIL LEE: On Saturdays, my little gang and I would head downtown to the Record Bar to check out the latest, and to hang out at the music stores. My main conduit for new music was Tommy Knowles, later known as River Cabbage. His folks died and left him some money, with which he immediately bought a motorcycle, a Stratocaster, two Silvertone Twin Twelves, and the latest Bob Dylan (we pronounced it Die-lan) records. He was the best bad influence ever. I was into music then, but through Tommy, I got into it deep.

DANIEL COSTON: *Describe your first band.*

PHIL LEE: The Tides, or some such thing. I think that was it or some such 6th grade kind of nonsense. Those were the days before the really cool names like Jade East and the Chesterfields took hold.

DANIEL COSTON: *How did you start playing with the Bondsmen?*

PHIL LEE: We were all at Northern High School together. Archie Thomas, Ken Haywood, Gene Galligan, John Santa, Hubert Deans and Jim Bowen, Jim Ward. How the conversation came up that we should start a band, I don't remember. I just remember the gig we did in the auditorium, the first one, and we were really good. We always seemed to be good when it counted.

collection of Phil Lee

The Bondsmen, 1967.

DANIEL COSTON: *What was music scene like in your town? Were there a lot of bands?*

PHIL LEE: There was a vibrant music scene in Durham. It was a big Chitlin circuit stop. For some reason, we never had a problem getting into the black shows, even at the Stallion Club. I got to see Joe Tex, James Brown. James opened for the Bondsmen once! We did a show with Sam & Dave, the Drifters. Anybody that we could see, we saw. I can't believe my Ma would drop us off at some of those places. In those days we played what was on the radio. So it was "She's About A Mover" into "Midnight Hour", followed by "Summertime". That's why the Bondsmen were at the top of the local garage band foodchain. We could do all that stuff pretty well.

There was the Checkmates, the Dukes of Durham, the Si-Dells. It was a friendly scene. WSSB played our records. Bill Day was our champion at the station. That really made us feel big-time. Buck Poe was the station manager. He treated us like musicians instead of bonehead kids, which we were.

DANIEL COSTON: *Did your classmates, and teachers look at you differently for being in a band?*

PHIL LEE: Being in a band, I got a pass on a lot of the crucial teenage bullshit. For one, being a leprechaun I couldn't go out for sports, and being a hippie was a one-way ticket to an ass-whupping. Being in a band, I got a complete free ride there, instant popularity.

I didn't appreciate it then, the time I spent on TV with Homer Briarhopper on "The Daybreak Show" may have been the most important for shaping my showbiz world approach. The suits. Showing up on time, fan mail. A lot of people in Raleigh and Durham tuned in before work or school to catch the farm news and hear a little real time country music, though we did a bit of everything.

DANIEL COSTON: *Tell me about some memorable shows that you played.*

PHIL LEE: The time we played the Forest Theater in Chapel Hill, and my girlfriend knocked me out for carrying on with another. All this happened during the show. The last thing I remember was her holding her little dog Puddin' in one arm, and swinging at me with the other.

Once we caused a sock hop to be canceled because we were drinking. That was a memorable one. We were known as "good boys", not like the Dukes of Durham. They were from Durham High School. They were really a great band, with Sam Rich and Billy Britt.

DANIEL COSTON: *In 1967, the band won a contract with the Chapel Hill-based AMH label by winning a statewide Battle Of The Bands competition at Dorton Arena, in Raleigh. The band's subsequent single, a cover of the Five Americans' "I See The Light," received a lot of airplay in the Triangle area. In 1984, Ken Friedman made this song his opening track on Volume One of his Tobacco A Go Go collection.*

PHIL LEE: Our first set went great. The second set, not so much. I think someone sabotaged our equipment.

DANIEL COSTON: *What do you remember about the recording session for "I See The Light"?*

PHIL LEE: Being real nervous. The night before I couldn't sleep. "Our Time To Try", the flip side, was written by Archie Thomas and John Santa the night before the recording session.

After the Bondsmen broke up, I moved to Chapel Hill and joined the Road Band. It was a psychedelic blues band and was really popular with the college girls there.

JAKE BERGER: I went to a festival held for the students of UNC with quite a few bands, and one of which was one named aptly, the Road Band. This is when I first became aware of Philip Pearson, whom the world knows as Phil Lee. During the show he pulled out all stops, mugging and pouting, using every trick from the Jagger moves book, and more. If you ever saw the Young Rascals on "Ed Sullivan", that is what his show brought to mind. Sort of a North Carolina version of the Rascals' drummer, Dino Dinelli. Jumping up from his kit and running in circles around it, doing the "Jagger Dance" and not missing a beat.

PHIL LEE: Don Dixon was in the Road Band. He was too wholesome, so he had to go! He'd fit right in, these days.

DANIEL COSTON: *The Counts IV were formed in 1965 by four musicians that were stationed at Seymour Johnson Air Force base, near Goldsboro. Their first single, "Listen To Me"/"Lost Love", was released later that year on the JCP label, A Raleigh-based label run by popular WPTF DJ Jimmy Capps. In 1966, after touring throughout the Southeast, the band's lineup changed, and they released their second single, "Spoonful"/"Where Are You", on CBS subsidiary label Date Records. The group would soon return to Goldsboro, where the lineup would go through more changes.*

Mike & The Dimensions also emerged from Goldsboro in 1965, formed from members of the Counts IV, the Cobras, and the Spectaculars. The quintet released one single, a cover of "Little Latin Lupe Lu." The single received airplay on local station WGBR. After the band broke up, some of the group's personnel formed a new version of the Counts IV, which later evolved into the Inexpensive Handmade Look. The band would release one single under this name, and count blues guitarist Mojo Collins among their ranks before breaking up in 1969.

The town of Lumberton jumped on the British Invasion bandwagon from the start. Bands such as the Motley Jesters, and the Reactions were popular throughout the area. The best known of the Lumberton bands was the Young Ones. Formed in 1965 by a group of friends from high school, the quintet of guitar players Carlton Warwick and Ronnie Baxley, Johnny Hayes on bass, Dickie Britt on organ, and songwriter Jimmy

Sossamon on drums, was an immediate hit at local Battle Of The Bands competitions. In 1966, the band released their first single, which featured "Too Much Lovin'". The song became a hit in different parts of the Southeast, and the band toured throughout the Carolinas.

The Young Ones developed a set that has known for its high-energy covers of British Invasion music. The band's finale often involved trashing their instruments on stage, before the Who popularized the stunt. The quintet made several TV appearances, and in 1967 released their second single, "Big Teaser", backed with "It's You". The band changed their name to the Psychic Motion for the single's release, to avoid confusion with another touring band named the Young Ones.

By 1968, the Young Ones were no more, and Jimmy Sossamon offered to manage another Lumberton group, called the Glory Cykle. Sossamon would later join the band on drums, so that drummer and vocalist Ken Allen could focus more on a being a frontman. By 1969, Sossamon, Allen and the rest of the group (guitarists Ralph Stevens and Jeff Hardin, bassist Grady Pope, and organist Rick Wilson) had shortened their name to Cykle, and recorded an album of Sossamon songs that they pressed and sold themselves.

The Monarks, from the Greenville, NC area, released one single in 1967. The single was recorded at Sound City Studios in Bailey, NC, which was also used by many regional touring groups. Both sides of the Monarks single were written by Chuck Eatmon. Also in the Greenville area, a group called Clear Blue Sky released one single at the Romat Label. The single was recorded at Pitt Sound Studios, which was located on the outskirts of Greenville. Romat was a subsidiary of Pitt Records, which released a number of soul and gospel records in the 1960s and '70s. Also recording for Romat were local groups the Scotsmen (not to be confused with Scotsmen from Cramerton), the Soul Twisters, and The Sound System.

Out in the Beaufort area, Huckleberry Mudflap formed in 1969, and quickly gained a following in Eastern NC. Appearances on Raleigh WRAL's Teen Screen TV show, and airplay for "Blue Surf" single on WMBL, WSFL and other local stations. The quartet toured throughout the region before disbanding in 1972. Other local bands in the Outer Banks area were the Kustoms, and the Reverbs.

The Symbols emerged in 1966 from former members of the Taxmen, one of Fayetteville's more popular groups. The Symbols released their lone single on the JCP label. Also recording for JCP was another popular Fayetteville band, the Marke 5. The band's lone single "Pay", backed with "The Leader," has appeared on a few popular compilations in recent years. Also recording for JCP were a number of Raleigh-based groups, including the Nightwalkers, Frankie & The Damons, and a host of other groups. Other groups from the Fayetteville area that recorded singles included the Psychotrons, and the Londons. The Soul Twisters emerged from Greenville, and while they were in fact an all-black soul quintet, their inclusion on Ken Friedman's Tobacco A Go-Go Volume 2 merits their mention in this book.

Other Eastern North Carolina bands that released singles between 1964 and 1969 included the Sands (from Raleigh), Vigilantes (from Apex), Turks (from Elkin), Pour Souls (Elon College), and the Jesters. Willie Lowery emerged from Robeson County, and led the multi-racial band Plant And See, one of the first racially integrated bands in the Southeast US. Their lone album was issued by White Whale Records (home to the Turtles, and many other acts) in 1969. Lowery would go on to lead many more acts, including the post-Plant And See band Lumbee, before he passed away in 2012.

By 1969, the Chapel Hill music scene was changing. The folk and bluegrass scene was giving way to new students, who had new ideas about the music they wanted to make.

TOM POPE: In my sophomore year at UNC, I put together a group with some other guys I knew from school. We were called Zero Davis, and we were Southern Rock. We played a lot. Peace rallies, jubilees, and backed up Chuck Berry one time.

DANIEL COSTON: *In 1969, Don Dixon began attending UNC-Chapel Hill, and would soon help create one of North Carolina's most popular bands throughout the 1970s. Dixon is still active today, with a remarkable list of credits as a musician, writer and record producer.*

DON DIXON: Growing up, I sang in the church choir and was enthralled with the records of my older sisters. Rock & Roll, R&B, Folk. I liked some Classical & Jazz LPs that my parents had but mine was not a musical family. We had a piano, a Hi-Fi. In 6th grade I began fooling around with my sister's guitar, but in 7th grade, right before the Beatles broke, I began playing trombone & learning a little about music. I taught myself bass listening to Meet The Beatles, the Peter & Gordon album, World Without Love, and the first Kingsmen LP.

DANIEL COSTON: *Was there ever a moment were you said, "Music is what I want to do"?*

DON DIXON: It always seemed like a path for me. I began making money as a working musician in my mid-teens, and never have had a real job.

DANIEL COSTON: *Describe your first band, and first shows.*

DON DIXON: My very first band was called The Racquets. Two trumpets, two alto saxes, two clarinets, trombone and drums. We played songs like "Java" (a hit for Al Hirt) and songs we composed, all instrumental. We didn't stay together long, but we did play a few paying shows. My next band was also initially instrumental, The Cavaliers. Organ, tenor sax, guitar, bass, drums. We played dances and beauty pageants all over SC, made regional Radio and TV appearances, an extremely successful band that stayed together throughout my high school years.

DANIEL COSTON: *Did you visit, or play in North Carolina before you went to UNC?*

DON DIXON: I grew up in Lancaster, SC, just an hour south of Charlotte. The Cavaliers performed in a massive dual state Battle Of The Bands, held for two days at the Charlotte Coliseum, where we got into the final round. Loonis McGlohon heard us there and was impressed by our repertoire of standards, and our relatively high level musicianship. He contracted us to be on a TV program he produced in Charlotte at WBTV called "The Newcomers". After that, he began hiring me to record and perform with him on a regular basis. I played all over the state of NC with Loonis in my teens, including a series of shows with the North Carolina Symphony doing a jazz concerto by Ned Rorem. Loonis was a significant mentor for me, and we stayed in touch over the years, in spite of the fact the he (in his words) "lost Don to Rock."

DANIEL COSTON: *What was the music scene in Chapel Hill like when you arrived there?*

DON DIXON: It was interesting, because of the times. When I got to town in 1969, the most successful band in the area was Doug Clark and The Hot Nuts. So many of the working bands were playing frat R&B a la Animal House, though this was years before that film. James Taylor had lived there just a few years before, so with his success being so current, a singer-songwriter culture was emerging. Plus, Woodstock had just happened the summer prior to my coming to UNC. I was already into Hendrix, and the West Coast scene as well as the British Invasion stuff, not to mention my jazz and standards background. My high school band, the Cavaliers, had developed into a Soul Revue with me as singer, so I also had been working up a sweat on the Stax and Atlantic catalogue.

Winston-Salem natives Robert Kirkland, Mike Greer and I all lived in the same dorm, Aycock, and within a few weeks had started a band by learning the import-only Black Sabbath LP, plus most of Abbey Road. But the impetus was always to play our own songs, and since the Vietnam War was not to be forgotten in those days, our first recording was an anti-war song written by Mike, sung by me called "Black Death". Having a record helped us forge a following in the thriving Winston-Salem coffee house circuit, and as the bands began proving that kids would come to shows, venues began to spring up. Other bands began to write their own songs. Robert and I began playing acoustically every Wednesday at a bar on Franklin Street called The New Establishment. Our acoustic persona was born.

DANIEL COSTON: *How did you come together with the other members of Arrogance?*

DON DIXON: As mentioned earlier, Robert, Mike and I were joined by Winston-Salem crony Jimmy Glasgow in the original line-up. Marty Stout, another Winston friend, joined us for many of our early recordings. After Mike and Jimmy left, Robert and I began to build a following in Chapel Hill with Marty on piano. We were joined on percussion by a friend I'd made while playing in the UNC Jazz Lab Band, Ogie Shaw. He played on our first LP, Give Us A Break, along with Charlotte session drummer Rob Thorne on three songs.

Ogie left, and was replaced by drummer Steve Herbert for our second album, Prolepsis. For our third record, our first national release, Rumors (on Vanguard), we hired Scott Davison, who remained with the band for the rest of its time together. Before signing to Warner-Curb and recording the album Suddenly [in 1980], we added guitarist Rod Abernethy, a friend from the Chapel Hill music scene.

DANIEL COSTON: *Did you have any long-term intentions for Arrogance in those early days?*

DON DIXON: Personally, I couldn't imagine being alive after age 25. I still can't. We just wanted to get in a van and play our songs, but we were pretty organized. We created an atmosphere that dictated a DIY aesthetic. Writing and singing and clawing, and scraping and pushing the envelope to reach more people. We didn't name ourselves Arrogance for nothing.

DANIEL COSTON: *How did the Chapel Hill scene change while you were in school?*

DON DIXON: The world changed, the music business grew, got more corporate. Chapel Hill reflected those changes, became less provincial. As I said, clubs sprang up, labels sprang up, bands got deals. Everyone had a dream.

DANIEL COSTON: *What effect did that time have on the rest of your life?*

DON DIXON: Obviously, when you work so closely with a small group of people for so long, over 13 years, those people have a massive influence. An influence that's impossible to quantify. The creative process is illusionary. Once you try to pin it down, it vanishes and shows up somewhere else. As a group, a band in the true sense of the word, we forged ahead against popular opinion, against tremendous odds, against authority and security. For those years we were together, the rewards were enough to keep us going, intrigued, fed, gas in the tank and strings on our guitars. I never really wanted much more, the lyrics to one of Robert's early songs, one that is still requested often, "Open Window" says it all.

*"I see a big house in the country
an open window, clouds in the blue sky
heavenly frame lying right there beside me
waking up smiling with the light in her eyes"*

1968 into 1969

JAKE BERGER: By the fall of 1967, going back to school was mandatory because of my being too young to quit, but it was a huge undertaking for me. I was simply not equipped to deal with a world of people that I didn't "get", and who didn't understand me. The only thing that kept me from being the punching bag of the Banlon bullies was the fact that I had a reputation of the most undesirable sort, a burden that while pretty much undeserved kept me safe from the young, would be "tough guys" in my age group.

I was left to my own devices and somehow ended up friendly with a kid in my grade at school named Bill Reynolds, who was already playing in a pretty good group known as the Durations during the early winter of 1968. Bill was responsible for my access to the Durations, because we were friends and because one of their guitar players had decided to switch to organ. He had acquired a brand new Vox Continental organ (Where did these kids get their money?), but he had a very nice early 60s Gibson SG special that I was welcome to play. For some reason, I opted to use the lead guitarist's Rickenbacker copy. It must have been because I related the Rick with the Brit bands that I loved so much. There was also a sax player that stayed with us for a few months before giving up the ghost. That band had an older kid from my school, Elmon May. Elmon could sing (we thought) like Otis Redding, and played a little trumpet, as well. In fact, I think before I left we were playing the song "Bend Me Shape Me", with its little trumpet intro.

The group consisted of, and these are the names I remember, Bill Reynolds on bass and vocals, Elmon May, lead vocals and trumpet, drummer Charley Hawkins, and older brother Roy on lead guitar and vocals, and then me on rhythm guitar, harmonica and vocals, plus the organ and sax men. This was the first band I played in that was truly a working band, and we played lots of private parties, Teen Cotillion dances. Teen Cotillion was a dance school that was also a "social status" thing for young well-heeled Myers Park kids. We played at the Charlotte Women's Club, and Eastway Junior High school dances. We also played maybe on a Sunday afternoon jam at a teen club on Wilkinson Boulevard called Joe's A Go Go, where later that year a friend and I got banned for having a six-pack of beer stashed on the floor of his dad's car. I'm sorry to say that by this time, playing music had taken a back seat to what was, without my being aware of it, fast becoming my favorite past-time. Getting stoned.

DANIEL COSTON: *1968 was the year that a generation's wide-eyed dreams ran into a darker reality. There were still highpoints to come into 1969, but the lows would come harder, and more prominently as the decade ended. For every Woodstock, there was an Altamont. Civil rights had begun to progress, but Vietnam continued unabated. "At least the Man can't take our music" was the slogan for one record label's promotion. For many, the world had become more "Us and Them" than the "What If's" of a larger, and better collective. But the music continued growing, and changing.*

1968 appeared to be the year that the Young Ages would break through nationally, after scoring a Decca contract by winning a Big WAYS Battle Of The Bands contact. The band then recorded two songs for Decca at Arthur Smith Studios.

JOHN BARKLEY: Roger Branch produced that for us on a four-track machine. We did "Reach Out (I'll Be There), and the Bee Gees' "In My Own Time". Pat Walters came up with the intro to "Reach Out", and I liked it so much, I kept it in the song.

BOB ROBINSON: It was the first time I had played a Hammond B3. I loved it.

JOHN BARKLEY: That was going to be the first band of our Decca contract, and then Vietnam came along, and we couldn't fulfill the contract.

RONNIE PHILLIPS: We were also supposed to go to California, as part of a talent contest that we'd won through Big Ways. But Mike went to Vietnam, and Dickie to Vietnam, and that was it.

BOB ROBINSON: The Decca tape was lost for decades, and it turned out that Melvin Cohen had a copy. Zan McLeod had ended up with Melvin's tapes, after Melvin died, and Zan said, "I'll come down and hand deliver this tape to you, so that nothing happens." We've since put it up on our website.

DANIEL COSTON: *Bands such as the Stowaways were also changing, giving way to a new wave of bands as the decade came to a close.*

TIM TATUM: One of our bandmembers had a religious experience. We were in a motel room after a gig, somewhere out of town, and we couldn't get him to come out of the bathroom, because he was having a meeting with Jesus. He had this spiritual awakening, I guess, and he wouldn't play music anymore. We'd have bookings, and he wouldn't show up. In 1968, I moved out of town. My dad got transferred, and that was it, for me.

BOYD ALBRITTON: I was progressing, and the band was not. One day, I just quit. I had five more gigs booked with the band, at the time, and I told that they needed to find another guitar player. I then took Bobby Donaldson's place in the Premiers. It was good for me to be behind Bobby Donaldson, because he would leave for another gig, and he'd say, "I know this guy," and I would get his old gig.

BARRY STACKS: I was convinced that doing something in music was in the stars for me, and Arnie continued managing, for me. In 1969, he called me and said, "I've got my own studio now. Are you still playing?" He had a studio in East Lansing, near Detroit, and we started recording. By that point, I'd had it with Arnie. I wasn't getting any money, so I severed ties with him. Around this time, I had this idea about a band that just recorded. Didn't play live, just record, and call the band Jules Verne. Over the next few years, I worked on Jules Verne songs.

DANNY HUNTLEY: The reason I quit the Paragons was I was given an ultimatum about either going to college or playing in the band. I was determined to become a physician, and was accepted at my dream school, Wake Forest University, so I had to quit.

DANIEL COSTON: *Back in Charlotte, Larry and Jimmy Duckworth continued playing under a variety of names.*

LARRY DUCKWORTH: One of the things that we did, and you think up the dumbest things when you are a kid, but when we'd been at other Battles of the Bands we'd heard the crowds yelling the names of the bands, and you couldn't do, "Abbadon! Abbadon! Abbadon!" Nobody even knew, I mean they called it, "Abandon, Abbadon, Abbadooboo". Nobody could pronounce that stupid name!

So we went, "Let's think of something that has the initials, "LSD", so the crowd can all start screaming, "LSD! LSD! LSD!!!!" Because that was the big thing. So we came up with, "Larry's Sound Department". And calling the band Larry's Sound Department had nothing to do with me, it was just so we could get the crowd screaming, "LSD!" and making a big commotion, and then the judges would go, "Man! These guys have got a big following!" And it worked beautifully!

JAKE BERGER: I just remember that when they would first come on when they were called Larry's Sound Department, the first thing you'd say was, "LSD!" They also went by the name of the West Side Melons. Those sort of names were floating around by then.

LARRY DUCKWORTH: What happened there is we needed a name. Remember the light show that I was talking about with all the lights? Well on the side of those crates, they were West Side Melon crates. Somebody came up to us and said, "What's the name of your band?" and we said, "Uhhhhhhh, West Side Melons!"

DANIEL COSTON: *Other musicians were beginning to help break down the lines of what was supposed to be black music, or white music.*

ZAN MCLEOD: I knew a musician named Purvis Lee, and he played downtown at some Holiday Inn, or something like that on a regular basis. I can't remember where it was, but it was on the other side of town. And I went in there, once in a while. He did a variety of stuff. He sang well, and he wasn't a bad guitar player. He did some of the Piedmont blues kind of stuff.

And then I met his son, who played bass, and got to be friends with him. And his son had a soul band, and I started playing with them! We played at some bad places! Those were some of the scariest gigs I ever did while playing with them. There were places in downtown Charlotte where only black people were allowed, and I played in some of those! It was quite and eye-opener! Some of those places didn't even open up until midnight!

I'd go in there at midnight and play until 4am, and serious junkies would wander in and transvestites, and stuff like that. Yeah, it was a scene! And there were some clubs out in North Charlotte that I'd play at and I'd be like the only white guy for miles around! I mean, it was an eye-opener.

It was similar to playing at Paul's Lounge, later on. You never knew when someone was going to open fire in there! We had to duck! I mean, seriously, at Paul's Lounge. I was playing with Munk in there, and somebody started shooting. In the club! Luckily, they were just shooting straight up in the air. They were drunk and stuff, and nobody got killed, but we had to dive and hit the stage! It was like the Blues Brothers!

DOUG JAMES: My first full-time professional gig was with the Marlboros, which was a beach music heading into Rock music sort of gig, and it had three or four black guys out front who could do the Temptations, Four Tops sort of routines, and I was in the band behind them. And the whole thing became more integrated as I stayed with them, and then the bands sort of changed over time. But yeah, traveling around with those guys was a very interesting experience.

I'm sure my parents were aghast, at the time, because it coincided with leaving high school. So that didn't go over well. Everything I did was "tolerated", and the worst I ever got was like, "Are you sure that is a good idea?" Or, "You really shouldn't do that because you just don't do that sort of thing." There was never any real discussion like, "You just do it" or, "This is the way it is". Or at least, that's not what I really accepted. But that's all I did. That's really all I've ever done for a living was music in one way or another. I threw papers when I was a kid. I think I had a two-week stint in an engineering company here, or something like that, and I think I washed windows for a couple of months for a service that did that, and lost my fear of heights. Cleaning the outsides of buildings. But those were very brief stints, and otherwise I have always done music in one way or another. So, I became very mercenary early on, I realized that if I play what they want to hear, they'll pay you. And so that was really why I was never in any bands that had really large "original" efforts. And that is a regret I have. I may still do it. I'm not done, yet.

That's when we started having the "freaks" and the "straights", I guess, for lack of better terms. The freaks were the people who were more counter-culture, and dressed and looked that way, and the straights were more straight and narrow. And it was a challenge musically, in that I was certainly playing music that was established rhythm and blues, Motown stuff was very straight and narrow. But we were really listening to the other stuff, and kind of slipping it in there every now and then. And then, eventually you had to have a different band. And that was also an era that you didn't have two bands. You played in one band. It was like one girlfriend, and one band. It is refreshing now that that's not the case. I don't know how I can really describe that issue, but music became more political, being affiliated with a cultural stream, with a political statement of sorts. We didn't think of it in terms of the word, political, we were too young, and that is just the way it was. I think that at that age and at that time, the word, politics just didn't come up.

It was also part and parcel of the breakdown of the black versus white cultures. The barriers between them, because at the beginning of the Rock era. The black music scene was totally segregated from the white. The record companies were different, the venues were different. The bands were not integrated, the record labels were integrated, that blew my mind when I found that out. And so when I started playing with the Marlboros, in the Seventies, it became a non-issue. Living with black folks, traveling with black folks, hanging out with black folks, dating black girls, whatever, it was a just whole different era. And I was a radical.

I remember that the thing that changed the music was that in late '69 and '70 when I first started playing with the Aqualads, it broadened my horizons just from Myers Park and that scene. That's when I started traveling all out of town and I played with guys from Garinger, from my neighborhood, so all of a sudden I was the one who was the "different one".

DANIEL COSTON: *In the summer of 1968, the nation was put on edge after the assassination of Martin Luther King Jr. Peace marches were as frequent as threats of violence. By this time, the Modulation Blooze Band was playing under the name Alairlura. After an article on the band ran in the Charlotte Observer, the trio was invited to play at one of the biggest rallies during that year.*

DENNIS EDWARDS: We were called Alairlura, by this point.

SHORTY NEHRENBERG: It means "coat of many colors". I think Phil got it from the Bible.

DENNIS EDWARDS: It was right after Dr. King had been killed. The girl that did a newspaper article on us, got us a gig playing when the Poor People marched on Washington. The poor people were marching from the Deep South all the way to Washington, and they stopped in Charlotte and they had the big thing out at the old Coliseum. So me, Shorty and Phil, our little three-piece band, we'd never been in a room that big. So we got on stage, and we were the only white people there. And we were only gonna do one song, I don't know if we even knew what we were gonna play.

SHORTY NEHRENBERG: We didn't. But we were gonna play something.

DENNIS EDWARDS: As we got on stage, Jesse Jackson started his speech. And he went on and on, and we were just standing right there behind him on the stage. I'll never forget it. He wound up introducing us, too!

SHORTY NEHRENBERG: So we're the only white people in there, and we're up on stage with Jesse Jackson.

DENNIS EDWARDS: We're standing right behind him, and I'll never forget that when he introduced us, I was playing bass and when I hit the first note on my bass I could hardly hear it!

SHORTY NEHRENBERG: We're just standing up there with our amps up on the stage at the Coliseum.

DENNIS EDWARDS: And I looked around at Shorty and said, "Let's just play, 'Help Me', that old blues song, and they ate it up!

SHORTY NEHRENBERG: Yeah, they loved it! They thought it was just great! They were coming up to us afterwards telling us how great it was!

JAKE BERGER: There was a lot of improv in that band.

SHORTY NEHRENBERG: That's right. Because we started listening to Cream, and we figured that's what they were doing, because we didn't know any better. We just figured if that's what they were doing, that's what we were gonna do. We had no idea that they actually knew what they were doing!

JAKE BERGER: In the fall of 1968, I was shipped off the Patterson private school, in Patterson, NC. This was a brutal place where they would force you into town for a skint-to-the skull haircut every two weeks, and hair being more important to me than school and certainly authority, I promptly loaded myself up on cough syrup and caught the first bus to Charlotte, and thus escaped the haircut and the school.

When I got back, I stayed on my own and spent the fall getting a buzz on and checking out the local bands. The G.B.U. were going strong, and August had moved to town, so there was no shortage of talent to inspire me.

About this time, I was told by Jimmy Duckworth that a fellow, Randy Hall (whom I kind of knew from around town) was looking for me, and wanted to play some music. After getting together, we formed a new band, the Red, White, and Defiantly Blues Band, with Gary Plavidal on drums, and a guy named Mike Smith on bass, Randy Hall on guitar and vocals, and me, guitar and vocals.

After a month, Gary stepped down, and drummer Don Tetreault joined. Then Mike left, and was replaced by Bill Roberts, and with a young guy, Brian Epstein on organ.

We played Small Faces, Spencer Davis, Rolling Stones, and a little Cream. We played at the teen club behind the church at the corner of Sharon and Providence Road, and at the Weddington County fair, where I borrowed Freddy Windham's bass amp to play guitar through. We got through about two songs and a drum solo (yes we played "Toad"!) before the folks in charge told us that we were taking punters away from the other booths, and were asked to shut it down. They paid us anyway, so all was good.

RANDY HALL: Jake Berger got me into the music. He was into the music, but he won't admit to being a hippy. And still won't.

JAKE BERGER: Around this time, I was refused re-entry back into A.G. to finish school, but was allowed into Randolph Junior High, and returned to the business of learning for a couple of months, until I resigned for good.

I had also started to hang around a house that a bunch of like-minded people had rented for $200 a month on Kingston Avenue, and that was Charlotte's first Hippie House. Or at least the first publicized one, and before the famous one on Central Avenue. There I was surrounded by folks a little older than me, but for the most part I was not treated like a "kid", and have great memories of them.

And then there was the infamous Ed Dotson. Ed was a strange guy from Shelby who was into all sorts of things, a truly strange guy but I had him pegged, and feel to this day that it was lots of theater with him. Ed later fell into drug addiction, and is in the Guinness Book Of World Records for the most bank robberies in a single day! He was dubbed "The Gentleman Bandit", and there is a movie about him in the works. Ed sold me the first LSD that I took, at that house.

Phantasmagoria membership card, 1969.

Very soon after that, I decided to hitch to Atlanta, and from there to Miami. While there, I went to the first Miami Pop Festival, in December of '68. I hitched back with a guy from Indian Trail that I had met while imbibing more acid in Coconut Grove, Florida. I stood in the sleet and cold for six hours in Savannah, Georgia, catching a raging case of tonsillitis in the bargain.

When I got home, I found that a whole new group of people were living on Kingston, and I didn't know anybody any more. This was the end of 1968, and after a short time a new "Hippie House" was established on Central Avenue.

DANIEL COSTON: *By 1969, some of the venues had begun to change. Rock festivals were beginning to be in fashion, and venues like the Fillmore West in San Francisco had given some the idea of a bigger place to showcase the music.*

Good Bad And The Ugly, 1969.

ZAN MCLEOD: Melvin's club, Phantasmagoria, really changed my life. He changed it, and renamed it after a while and called it Genesis. And that was out in Matthews. In fact there is a fish camp that is still in the same building. That building had so much good music in it over about a two or three year period there. It was incredible. It was amazing!

DEBBY DOBBINS: Phantasmagoria was the awesomest place of all! Good Bad And The Ugly were together at that point and they were practically the House Band over there. And I was there every single night. Every single night I was over there. God, was it a such great place!

RANDY HALL: Phantasmagoria was the first real rock club in town. We'd had the Purple Penguin in high school, but it was pretty redneck. Melvin Cohen, and twelve or thirteen other people went in together. They got a lot of bands through a booking agent in Atlanta.

ERIC ROBINSON: I saw a lot of great bands out of Phantasmagoria. Good Bad And The Ugly. There was Hector, which featured Tim Moore. There was an amazing group called the Booger Band, a three-piece out of Atlanta. Seeing them play was a true experience. They had a Battle Of The Bands quite often.

JAKE BERGER: I was hanging out with this one band called Speed Limit 35 at Phantasmagoria, and we were having a good time. And I said, "Why don't you do this last set with no clothes on?" And the drummer said, "Yeah, let's all do it!" And they did!

DANIEL COSTON: *Other venues in Charlottte were changing themselves for the younger audiences.*

collection of Zan McLeod

Salvation, 1970.

ROB THORNE: I was moving away from what the Catalinas had done in that scene and going to this other kind of scene of Rock & Roll stuff. So, there was a transition right then. And the Cellar was a big part of that at that time. That was probably the best venue in town for bands. The Catalinas would play it on Sunday nights, or the Tams would come in on Sunday. A lot of good, great recording bands, like maybe Sam & Dave, or people like that.

Sunday nights at the Cellar were gangbusters. They'd sell out of beer. There'd be a thousand people down there, they'd be out in the parking lot with a line going out the door, and they'd be hot and sweaty and it was just a madhouse, and so much fun! You could barely move and everyone was trying to dance to the bands. There was a little stage back up in the corner.

And then, in '70, I was playing with Salvation and we played the Cellar. So, the psychedelic and more Rock & Roll bands had taken over the Cellar, and not necessarily the Beach bands. I don't know where the beach bands were playing, but it wasn't places like the Cellar.

LARRY SPRINKLE: I would go and see bands at the Cellar. I saw the Allman Joys there, in 1969. Everybody played the Cellar. A lot of the beach music bands played there, but a lot of rock bands played there. Larry Presley was the guy that owned the Cellar, at that time. He had Kaleidoscope Productions, which promoted a lot of shows, and he bring in these band that were just starting on their way up, and they'd play the Cellar. That's why they started calling themselves the World Famous Cellar. You also had Phantasmagoria, Midnight Sun, Milestone, Purple Penguin. Later on, there was Randy's, the Treehouse, Paul's Lounge.

ERIC ROBINSON: The first head shop that opened up in town was Shreed Holding Company. They used to have concerts in the parking lot. I bought my first rolling papers there. It was in an old gas station. Later, another place, Chronosynclasticinfindibulum opened. That place opened up next to where the Double Door Inn is now.

RANDY HALL: We started a band called Spare Change. All of the hippies would come up and say, "Spare change?" They were always looking for money, so we called it "Spare Change."

ROB THORNE: We played a Battle Of The Bands at Freedom Park. It was like the New Mix and The Paragons, in the summer of 1968. I came home and took a leave that weekend so I could play in that thing. I think it was on a Sunday, and I don't remember who all was there, but yeah, The New Mix did play. It might have been something that Melvin Cohen was doing. And I was wearing a wig. I didn't have any hair because I was in the Army. I was wearing a blonde wig, with a Beatley look. There is a picture of it. I saw it a while back.

JAKE BERGER: I remember Johnny Hostetler playing with August out at Freedom Park. August was made up of former members of the Villagers. I remember they did, "Ain't No Telling" by Jimi Hendrix, and he went running out into the audience. These girls, high school and college girls, they'd never seen anybody like him. Hair out to here, and he went running out in the audience, and they were running from him! Like, he was just so scary! They had a drummer that would just sit there doing rolls with one hand. That was the first time I ever saw anyone do that.

DANIEL COSTON: *By this time, one section of Freedom Park had become popular as a place where people could gather without too many hassles. This part of the park became known as "Hippie Hill."*

JAKE BERGER: I had started hanging out at Freedom Park around this time. The year before, the crowd had started with a small group of people hanging out on the hill by the old Exxon building, on Woodlawn Road. The group consisted of folks like Shorty Nehrenberg, Dennis Edwards, Carla Frieze, and Carla's boyfriend, Tom West. They would gather there from time to time, and play guitars and groove. The group moved from there to the island near the pond in Freedom Park, growing in numbers as it did. The everyday public, who had never before exposed to the newly christened counter-culture, would pass by with a bemused expression on their mugs.

CHUCK WHITAKER: I started coming to the Park in the spring of '67. Originally, it was veterans and dissatisfied young people. Vietnam, and the anti-war movement helped to cement a lot of people together. The brutality of the time was pretty bad. I slept here a lot of times. The crowds went on Hippie Hill went from a handful of people to seven, eight hundred in the process of a year. And then we had another boom in crowds, after Woodstock.

DON TETREAULT: Me and a friend made it up to Woodstock. We made it there early Sunday, through Sunday, and had Jimi Hendrix wake us up the following morning, and then it was time to go. We didn't think of it as being history. It was more like a big convention. It was muddy, so you wore jeans and a t-shirt. You were tired, and people were passing out sandwiches. I traded a bologna sandwich for a peanut butter and jelly sandwich, because if was more filling. I hitchhiked from here to Woodstock. I didn't tell my parents where I was going. My parents saw reports of the festival on TV, and my dad said, "I bet that's where he is." I remember walking up the main road, and people were out in their front yards, and cars were just everywhere.

JAKE BERGER: I remember walking around Charlotte, trying to find a ride up to Woodstock.

DON TETREAULT: I also went to the Atlanta Pop Festival. That was great. I remember closing my eyes during Led Zeppelin's set, and they sounded just like their first album. Spirit was really good, as well.

DONNY FLETCHER: I remember hearing Led Zeppelin's first album in 1969, and realizing that it was coming from a whole different place. I won't say it was better, but it was different.

DANIEL COSTON: *As the decade ended, new bands that would carry the Charlotte music scene into the next decade. New bands such as Mynd Garden, and Sugarcreek began to emerge. By the summer of 1968, Pat Walters had left the Paragons, and was in search of something new. That search would eventually lead him to his friends Phil Lowe, Henry Steele and Bobby Pace, who together would form the Good Bad And The Ugly, one of Charlotte's most popular bands as the 1960s turned into the 1970s.*

PAT WALTERS: My father got a job in Greensboro and my mother had remarried and moved to South Carolina. So, I didn't want to go, so I stayed here. I made it somehow.

DANIEL COSTON: *So the music actually helped to support your life.*

PAT WALTERS: Yeah. That was the only way I earned any money. I wasn't getting any support. I mean, I didn't expect any.

I think we spend all of August [of 1968] putting GBU together. I also went with some guys from The Villagers, so they had some gigs that they still had to do. The Villagers had broken up, but they still had these gigs, and here I was 15, maybe 16. I went to the Deep South with these guys in the back of a station wagon that had no air conditioning. But they felt that I was good enough to play with them. And they were maybe ten years older than me!

Everybody knew who all the people were in the pictures of the band, and they said, "Well, there was a car accident", because they had a female vocalist, who was not there, and they had a great guitarist, who was much more experienced than me who was not there, so they said there'd been a car accident. And we also played some little bar gig in Charlotte. I'm sure I wasn't old enough to be there. We rehearsed, and went to Mississippi. It was a great experience for me. And we went to Atlanta and they really had some hippies down there! How can I get my hair as long as they have their's?

Getting hooked up with an agent for GBU was good. They kept us busy. Of course, there was a lot of stuff with going to the colleges, to frat parties. Ted Hall, or whoever the agent was, they got us a frat party. I remember that there were some alumni there and they were more beach music oriented. Short-haired dudes, and they didn't want nothing to do with hippies and I remember having beer thrown at us from people like that. And that kind of sucked. Belmont Abbey had some good gigs. They had a big room.

But there were also events that would just have a big concert out in a quad, or something. So that was a new thing for us, and we got a good reception playing those things. We played up at Davidson College, and it wasn't like the gigs now where you worry about playing dance music. You just jammed for half an hour as long as you were good and people liked it, you'd get gigs. So there were a lot of things like that that really paid well. And were pretty classy gigs for us guys.

JAKE BERGER: I saw GBU open for Canned Heat at Park Center. They were really dramatic. Instead of just walking on stage and plugging in, they had

collection of Gill Vanderlip

Pat Walters and GBU are interviewed by Jimmy Kilgo, 1968.

the curtain closed. The curtain opened, and there's Pat with his striped bell-bottoms, and his vest and a furry schirpa hat, and just hair down to here. He was like, 17, and as the curtain opened, they started playing "Repent Walpurgis." They just had more showmanship.

DAVE LONG: GBU played my wedding, in 1969. They did the Procol Harum song, "Repent Walpurgis."

JAKE BERGER: When the "Hippie House" on Kingston Avenue was closed down by the police (and popular consensus), a group of people rented a house on the corner of Central Avenue and Hawthorne Lane. This house became infamous for harboring runaways and much drug use. At least once a week, the police would come knocking and haul away some kid who was either visiting just for fun, or one who had actually run from an unhealthy environment at home. The two people that were instrumental in maintaining this residence, Marvin and Kathy Sparrow, had recently popped up on the scene. It was rumored that Kathy was a descendent of President Taft (her maiden name was Taft), and that she was filthy rich. I don't know if that was true, but if so, it's kind of ironic as she was a self-proclaimed communist, and later they started a quasi-commie organization called the Red Worms, and had a house where they all lived in the upscale neighborhood of Dilworth.

At the house on Central, I took a ton of acid and speed, combined. The effects on my thinking were immense, but also unnoticeable to me. I just didn't see it coming, but come it did in a big way. First, I came down with hepatitis, as did many of my friends. We were teenagers and didn't have a clue as to the damage that we were inflicting upon ourselves. On top of that, we would take as much of whatever drug coupled with alcohol, or anything else without any thought to what we were taking, or how much. About this time, a friend and I hitch-hiked to Miami (this was the second time for me), and after a few days of hanging out in Coconut Grove we enjoyed a night of tripping, only to be hauled in by the police while walking down the streets of Coral Gables, Florida at 7 in the morning. I was sent to the Miami version of Jackson Training School (a reform school in Concord, NC) to wait for my parents to send for me. After a week of defending my ass from kids that were too old and too crazy to be there, my father finally sent the cash to bail me out, so back home again I went. I left soon after, and ended up living in Veteran's Park, on Central Avenue. The Sixties were done, my life of exploration and freedom was done, and sadly the music that had fired my imagination and fueled my rebellious youth was done, as well.

By the end of '69, I had lost interest in making music and was starting the downward spiral. Like the song said, "High water everywhere, things is lookin' grim 'round here". Well, that's the way things look to me. By 1969, I remember being smothered. A feeling of being perplexed and mad as slowly I came to the realization that everything had just heaved a mighty shift, or at least a slight side-step. That feeling of everything being "up for grabs" as far as adventure, or fun, such as it was (or had been up till now) was flying away fast. I was erratic, like a hubcap that has come off and goes "skittering" down the road.

The summer of 1969 was as hot as any on record, and it was also then that I developed allergies to pollen, and the other things that blow around in the great outdoors. All summer I had problems with my breathing, and the massive doses of the lysergic that most everyone I knew, myself included, had consumed over the last year or so had started to give us all a dark brooding frame of mind.

The epiphany that the worm had turned came on the July 4th holiday, stretched out in the blistering heat of the Atlanta Speedway at the first Atlanta Pop Fest. On

July 3rd, I had hitched and been given a ride by a family of teenagers from Chapel Hill, NC, being escorted to the festival by their mother. They were very kind and had stopped at a campground that evening, asking me to be their guest. As we sat around the fire that night, a news flash came on their transistor radio telling us that the most creative and the most dissipated member of the Rolling Stones, Brian Jones, had drowned in his swimming pool about eight hours before.

It came to me in a flash, all the things that had influenced me from the way I thought to the way I looked, and the music I loved had suddenly become obsolete. I remember having a very clear thought of, "How did it come to this?" and so this is a pretty good semblance of the time, and of the most important influence in my life, the music.

It's important to keep in mind that while during that time everybody in my world was being influenced by what ever influenced everybody else from the age of pre-teenism to full blown teen agers to young adults. As the decade wore on, adult culture was influenced by us. Also, in order to keep it in perspective, it is a good idea to see that even though Charlotte was small in the 1960's, and the South was not looked upon with much enthusiasm in more sophisticated environs, every bit of youth culture that happened in the meccas of say, London or Los Angeles, happened here, there, and everywhere else. Just slower to happen, sometimes, but by the time it did you got a mutated version, which made for some pretty unique characters. But the most unique and powerful mutation was the music and music scene, not only here but also throughout the south. It is also of utmost importance to be aware that there was a huge and vibrant music scene going on, and most were teen bands and there were many venues for them to show their stuff. Make a hell of a noise, chase teenage girls, show off their "Mister High Style" kicks, lids, and duds and that for a short while, we had it all.

To the Seventies … and Beyond

JAKE BERGER: It was all really only there for five or six years, and now is gone. Never to be repeated, all in a half of a decade for all that was to come after would be tainted by "business", the companies having discovered by the end of the decade just how much money there was in the exploiting of a youth culture that was centered around the music. The next decade would turn out some of the worst, most contrived pop music of all times, if you don't agree, I will say only this. The Eagles. I rest my case. How could this not happen, when by now the focus was not on the joy of creating or of being young, but on chart position and limos?

The music by now had changed into the music of the next decade and no longer held my interest, and the local teen band scene all but dried up. However, there were several small venues that carried the mantle for the next generation of players, and fostered a second wind in Charlotte during the 70's. The Foxhole had Charlotte muso Woody Mitchell getting his chops together. Woody was a Vietnam vet, had been injured by a grenade, and had been hospitalized in San Francisco in 1967. He got discharged, and then took up guitar. He was in the right place at the right time, hung with Shorty Nehrenberg, Dennis Edwards and Ronnie Loflen while they were there. He eventually made his way home to Charlotte forging his own niche in the musical landscape of the town.

In the early 70's came the Yellow Rose, and there the return to roots music in a country vein started to germinate, led by Woody and others, as the Double Door Inn did with Lenny Federal. By the middle of the decade, the Double Door started bringing in some of the remaining blues players along, with the new white bluesmen (the Nighthawks, Bob Margolin, and Arhooly), along with a handful of like-minded clubs nationwide, saved the blues from extinction.

The scene picked up again in the late 70's and early 80's with the infusion of punk rock, and then what was dubbed "alternative rock". A whole new crop of young folk were now at the forefront and as it should be, started carving a place for themselves in the scheme of things, along with new clubs for them to play in. The one thing yet to be repeated is the glut of youngsters still in their teens, and by necessity, an abundance of clubs geared especially for them. It is my hope that someday somehow the magic will return. It won't in my lifetime, but as long as it does in somebody's lifetime, all is as it should be.

DANIEL COSTON: *After spending much of the previous two years with the Army, Rob*

Thorne returned to Charlotte in 1970 to find a new direction.

ROB THORNE: When I came home that summer, in 1970, the first thing I did was, there was an anti-war march from the induction center on Pecan Avenue down to Veteran's Park, on Central Avenue. There were several hundred people, and I put on a uniform and got a parade drum and we marched all the way down to Veteran's Park. Jon Mullis and David Long played, a bunch of folk people got up and sang protest songs. It was all about protesting the war in Vietnam. WBTV was there. TV stations were taking pictures of us. The FBI was there taking pictures of us. The CIA, all of the organizations were there.

DANIEL COSTON: *Soon after, Rob Thorne joined forces with Zan McLeod and Munk Fellows in Salvation.*

ROB THORNE: [Salvation] was a great band! It was solid hard-ass Rock & Roll! Psychedelic as can be, jamming like crazy! The two guitar players, Munk and Zan together were a killer combination! And we played on college campuses, we played clubs around the state, like the Cellar, and the End Zone up in Greensboro was one of the other places. We played places like that. We would play college fraternity houses, and stuff like that. We'd go down in the basement of fraternity houses and set up, and start just blowing the damn windows out!

And most people had no idea what we did. We didn't realize how powerful it was. And most of the kids liked it. Except every now and then we'd get a negative reaction from a fraternity house that was not expecting what we were doing. Of course if they objected, it didn't matter because we didn't give a shit! We would play what we were gonna play, anyway! We were very In Your Face, and not angry but, you know, we had an attitude like, "If you don't like it, then leave!" But and it was just flat out Rock & Roll!

DANIEL COSTON: *After Salvation, the band evolved into another quartet, with Cliff Davis on bass, called Hummingbird. Meanwhile, Steve Stoeckel would join forces with Larry and Jimmy Duckworth, Tim Moore and Debby Dobbins in Eros.*

PAT WALTERS: GBU broke up in 1970. We reunited under another name, briefly, with me, Phil and Henry Steele in 1972. In 1970, I was asked by David Brown of the New Mix to go to New York to play on the Jeremiah album. Karl Jarvi was on bass. Phil Lowe, who was already living in New York, played on some of the tracks. Also, Denny Seiwell, future member of Wings, was on drums. Dave Spinosa, one of the guitar players on Paul McCartney's Ram album, was also on guitar. David Brown didn't want to play out much, but we did play a few live gigs with David Brown, Karl, me and Johnny Pace. Before getting back together with Phil and Henry. I also played with David Floyd in the Flares, and with Johnny Pace in some other short-lived bands.

DANIEL COSTON: *In 1978, Rob Thorne would join up with Stoeckel, Walters and Jake Berger to form the Spongetones, a band that embraced the music that had sparked them all to play. After Berger moved away for a short time, the band took on guitarist Jamie Hoover. All those years later, after twelve albums of original music, and touring internationally, the quartet is still going string to this day.*

JAKE BERGER: I don't really feel like the Spongetones actually became the "Tones" until they ended up with Jamie Hoover. Yes, I played the first two gigs with them, but Jamie was the right guy for the job. He just hadn't "entered the movie" yet. What actually happened was that I booked a gig at a place called the Hitching Post in the late 70's. It was a "throw together" gig, which means there were no rehearsals, and everybody just showed up for the job and sort of figured out what songs they collectively knew. We got through that, and then either Pat Walters, or maybe I booked a show for the Double Door Inn. For this gig, we rehearsed two or three times, and that was when Steve kind of said, "I know all these Beatle songs", and that's what we played at the Double Door.

The next day, I went to New York with Danny Baker (later known as Unknown Hinson) and stayed there for a month or two. When I came back, they had kept going with the Tones thing, using another guy, and then the next time I saw them they had Jamie, and the rest is history. So really, I can't say, "I started the group". However, I had been booking Throw Together gigs for a couple of years before this, under the Spongetones name, so I guess I did contribute that. Perhaps my contribution was as a catalyst. The type of songs that I have written would never have fit in that "pop" mold, and whatever they have done was done solely by the efforts of those four guys. They certainly didn't need any outside help.

DANIEL COSTON: *Some always ask when the 1960s truly ended. For some in Charlotte, it ended in the summer of 1970 with the Love Valley festival, a large gathering that attracted some of the bad vibes that was infecting many festivals by this time.*

ERIC ROBINSON: The Love Valley Festival was a festival held at a horse ranch just on the other side of Statesville. It was over-run with bikers, Hell's Angels, musicians and hippies. It was a good show. Terry Reid was awesome. They had a mosh pit in front of the stage, and when the Allman Brothers walked offstage, and people started throwing mud at them.

ZAN MCLEOD: And then Melvin [Cohen] got busted in Love Valley, and that really pissed him off. It got on his record. He got pulled over, and he barely got off without serving any jail time. He got probation, and all that stuff. Love Valley was a weird festival. And yeah, at Love Valley somebody got killed! Some biker got murdered. It was kind of the mini-Altamont of North Carolina. They had roadblocks set up, like, so that when you came out of the festival, the local redneck cops said, "We're gonna get us some hippies!" And they just started busting everybody. Just pulling people over for no reason, and they started searching everyone's cars. And they did that to Melvin. That was a real bummer.

RANDY HALL: The house band [at Phantasmagoria] was Good Bad And The Ugly, and after they started touring more, my band started playing more out there. About a week or two later, there was a big drug bust. Some people that the police had been following got busted out there with a whole bunch of people. It was really chaotic. About a month or two later, Melvin had to close the club.

DOUG JAMES: The band that I was playing with was called Trick. It was Tom Drake on drums, and a guy named Junior Smith. That was just so crazy, that was it. At that point it was so crazy and I got ripped off, all sorts of crazy stuff. And Ernie Ferreri had introduced me to classical guitar playing. So I just did a 180 and started practicing four or five hours a day, and started doing that. It was partly a reaction. Because you could do it by yourself and it was no crazier than I was. So yeah, that was acceptable. And it was also just that I'd been trying to play more progressive to rock music and classical was extremely complex, and so it appealed to me in that way. And so that is what my career has largely been since that time.

DON TETREAULT: I learned that I couldn't be stoned every night to play for a living. I couldn't be stoned, and play for three hours a night. You had to be up and down, and stop and start at the drop of a hat. Know what verse it is, stop on three, hit on four, end on one, go into another song. And understand the song. You didn't think about it that much, when you were jamming. It wasn't work for me, but I had to be a professional.

JAKE BERGER: I cannot in good conscience recommend drugs, including alcohol, having seen firsthand the pitfalls. At the same time, I cannot tell anybody how to live their life, especially after a lifetime of going my own way, but I can tell anybody that cares about my own experience, and lots was not good, to the point of being a horrid experience because of the self-imposed hardship that comes with this type of abuse. I will also say that because I was able to break free of it, everyday I am grateful not to have that particular millstone around my neck to add to the weight of all the other ones that have been dragged around for all those years.

DANIEL COSTON: *David Floyd continued playing with various versions of the Flares until the mid 1970s. Various lineups included future disco sensation Alicia Bridges, and singer Diane Brodie. Floyd and Brody would eventually form Brodie's Down Home Cooking, with Rob Thorne and Bobby Donaldson, which would become another popular Charlotte act during the 1970s. David has since gone to play with numerous musicians from around the country, and in 2011 oversaw a reunion concert and DVD for many bands from the Gastonia area.*

DAVID FLOYD: when I was with The Flares, the first gig we played was at a fraternity party in Chapel Hill. And it was Diane's first gig with us. She disappeared right before we were supposed to play, and then she came out completely wrapped up in an American flag! That was very odd for 1973. It was not cool to be doing no American flag like that! She freaked out the fraternity, and that's about all I remember about that night.

DANIEL COSTON: *On the radio side, there was a shift going on from the Top 40 sounds of AM radio, to the album-oriented sound of FM radio. FM would soon outshine AM, and change the balance of how people discovered new music. After three years in Memphis, Larry Sprinkle returned to Charlotte and oversaw the transformation of WROQ. He went on to work at Big WAYS, and been on television with Charlotte station WCNC for nearly 30 years.*

LARRY SPRINKLE: WROQ was one of the original Album Rock stations in the country. I was the program manager, and Stan Kaplan came to me and said, "There's a new format called Album Rock." I told Stan that we didn't have any of the time. At the time, WROQ was an automated FM mono station. It was the beginning to FM radio. I told Stan, "You can't buy these records in Charlotte. There's only one place we can go. Peaches Records, in Atlanta". He gave me a check, and I flew to Atlanta, walked in to Peaches and bought something like 450 albums. I took them back to Charlotte, and two days later we went on the air. That was the beginning of WROQ as a rock station. This was in 1973. We were programmed oldies during the day, and from 7pm to 6am, we were live Album Rock.

DANIEL COSTON: *However, not everyone was happy with the shift to FM radio, and the new direction of Rock music during the 1970s.*

JAKE BERGER: When I was a kid and just starting to get the idea that I wanted to be a musician as a vocation, I was totally inspired by radio. AM radio, that is. Radio, unlike most of the south, was not still segregated and you might hear the latest from Stax, or Buck Owens' latest, backed up by a new one from the Beatles or the Stones. This type of format really made radio exciting and there was because of this method of programming, a huge variety of different groups and artists that were exposed to the youth of the day. The reigns of control started to slowly tighten during the mid 1960s, and then very quickly started chocking the life out of radio.

All of a sudden, you had the DJ's now being as laid back and as "hip" as they could fool you into believing they were, droning on endlessly in that irritating monotone voice, that has now become the standard, about absolutely nothing and then spinning the latest by the likes of Grand Funk Railroad, who I hated. And not just a single, an idea whose time was just about up, but whole horrible sides of LP's. Because of this, albums were now the standard for radio giving us hours upon hours of music in which the focal point was no longer the written song itself, but the endless and mind-numbing "noodling" of the recorded musicians.

I attribute to the homogenization of pop music and because of that, the homogenization of youth culture all due to the inception of FM as a format for the music of young people. Now, 50 years later that unexciting format is still with us with a whole slew of stations spewing forth all manner of generic music from generic country to generic rock to Celine Dion, and to this very day you can find any number of FM stations that are still airing the same sounds they did 35 years ago, as if we haven't heard enough "Stairway To Freebird"!

DANIEL COSTON: *On December 22nd of 1973, the Double Door Inn opened next to the Chronosynclasticindibulum, and just across from Central Piedmont Community College. The venue quickly became a home for many acoustic musicians around the city, and would eventually bring in numerous blues and rock bands. Jon Mullis, Lenny Federal, David Floyd, the Spongetones. Many of the people mentioned in this book would also find their way to the venue, which still operates to this day.*

As the 1990s dawned, the internet began to fill up with postings about bands in the 1960s, and the recordings that they left behind. A new generation of listeners began to search out bands that they heard on compilations of garage rock bands, as they were beginning to be called, or reading about in fanzines North Carolina bands were no excep-

tion. As of this writing, the "Abba" single that Tim Moore sold in the hallways of his school for two dollars now sells for upwards of $1,800. Due to the limited number of their printing, the Stowaways album sells for upwards of $800, as do most albums on Justice Records.

KEN KNIGHT: I started getting letters from people about the early '90s. People from Michigan started writing me, wanting to buy copies.

TIM TATUM: Later, this company called Collectibles bought up the Justice archive, and put out the Stowaways record on CD. They called me and said that they were going to put the record out on CD, and I said, "Why do you want to do that?" They said, "It's a classic of the Garage Rock genre." I wrote one song on there, and I have gotten some royalty checks from them, the biggest one being for $7.25.

BARRY STACKS: The Grifs songs are on a whole lot of compilation CD. Because of that, they get played all over the world. I've gotten emails from Japan, in Australia, England. I talked to one guy in England that told me that he played "Catch A Ride" in his car while driving through the streets of London at 100 miles an hour, because his wife had to get to the hospital because she'd just gone into labor. Writing is writing, whether it's music, or literary. You have to hone your craft, and pull words out of mid-air. I'm learning now that I'm visited by the same cosmic mailman that I was visited by when I was writing music.

DANIEL COSTON: *Many other bands would also find their way back together via the internet. In 2006, the members of the Young Ages got back in touch via email, and banded together once more. The original sextet played together again until 2000, when guitarist Dickie Carrigan had to bow out, due to claustrophobia caused by his time in Vietnam.*

JOHN BARKLEY: Vietnam got him twice.

DANIEL COSTON: *The band currently continues on with original members Johnny Barkley, Ronnie Phillips, and Mike Raper.*

JAKE BERGER: In the 1990s, after I had re-set the workings of my life, and gotten interested once again in making music, I was introduced to Phil Lee, and ended up playing with him for a number of years. Because of Phil, I was able to do what I had dreamed of when I was but a lad. I got the opportunity to travel the United States, as well as playing in England, and Scotland. With Phil, I ended up playing the Cavern, in Liverpool. Of course, the original Cavern had been leveled in order to build a parking lot, and the club was moved next door. But still, the Cavern! To my mind, Phil is one of, if not the premier songwriter in the country today. He tends to use all of his influences to his advantage without aping them. He can rock like the Stones when they actually could, and be as "pensively introspective" and as "sensitive" as any of the singer songwriters of today, without sounding like a jaded Nashville songster that has spent to many hours writing "jingles" in order to survive. I am proud to have had the chance to play his songs, and of his friendship.

DANIEL COSTON: *Jake Berger stayed in touch with many of the musicians from the Charlotte scene, including Johnny and Bobby Pace. Sadly, both Pace brothers passed away before the Paragons and "Abba" began attracting a whole new audience.*

JAKE BERGER: Bobby Pace was an easy going and quiet kind of guy who was more at home in his dad's electronic repair shop, at Ajax Television Service, than on the bandstand. Every time Johnny comes to mind, I am saddened by the loss. Johnny was a fine musician who's style of drumming was defined by the music of the 60's, and I always felt he was a little lost as that music passed out of popularity. Had he survived, he would have seen that what goes around indeed comes back again, and would have found his niche, as have many of us that didn't quite feel like wrapping our heads around the latter-day styles.

DANIEL COSTON: *Larry Duckworth continued playing with his brother Jimmy, as well as with several Rock and Jazz groups across North Carolina. Jimmy Duckworth's passing in 2010 did not allow us to get his own words into this book, but his spirit continues on. This book is dedicated to Jimmy Duckworth, Johnny and Bobby Pace, Melvin Cohen, and everyone of that time that carried on the music.*

LARRY DUCKWORTH: Playing with my brother was awesome. One, because we could just share all of this stuff and he could teach me about what he was doing and I would tell him about what I was doing. We had great arguments, you know, about stuff! We'd spend lots of time saying stuff like, "That tune shouldn't be that fast! What makes it good is it's slower!" One of my favorite ones was we argued about, I think it was "Honky Tonk Women", by the Rolling Stones. On the record of course it's real deliberate, and they were always on me because I'd always get real excited and play it fast! "You gotta play it slower! That's what makes this tune!" And we go to see the Rolling Stones and they played it ten times faster than they did on the record! And we go, "Well, shit! What were we arguing about? What was the big damn deal? I guess we don't know shit!"

We All Shine On — Final Thoughts on the 1960s

JAKE BERGER: I would love to see a resurgence of the teen club culture. I feel that there are so many kids that don't have a venue to play when they should. I imagine there a few institutionalized programs like art schools, and such that might encourage the development of a talent, but without the actual experience of a cross pollination of musical ideas and the opportunity to fall flat on your face publicly, get up. Dust yourself off and give it another go, growing stronger in the process. There won't be as much of that inner strength that enables one to weather the storms of momentary disillusionment, and temporary failures that ultimately lead to stronger conviction in ones musical endeavors and perchance success, and maybe, just maybe, the "new" spawning ground of such activities will once again be the ever present neighborhood garage.

DANIEL COSTON: *What is the legacy of the music of the 1960s? In Charlotte, in North Carolina, or anywhere else? Its greatest legacy may be that it changed many lives for the better, and continues to steer others into a lifetime of playing music. Nearly everyone that we've spoken to for this book is still performing on a regular basis. The hope of any art form is that it reflects something about what the artist was going through, and in turn affects the viewer, or listener into some sort of response. Through multiple generations, the music and the people, as John Lennon once said, shine on.*

TOM POPE: There were a lot of places to play. There were a lot of teen clubs. No smoking, no drinking, and hardly ever any trouble. The kids just wanted to dance. I remember one time at the Web, we had over 500 people, and they just danced all night. There were a lot of opportunities. You got together some friends, put together a band, and go get some gigs. You had that base back then that was so positive. There was nothing negative about it.

ZAN MCLEOD: A lot of really original and creative things were going on in those days. And the fans were really different. To me, these days it is just getting harder and harder to be different, and there were a lot of original and creative ideas floating around back in those days because it really hadn't been done. All the sounds that we take for granted now were just being invented back then.

DEBBY DOBBINS: How happy it was! How much fun it was despite people who tried to make it "not fun". It was a very innocent time. And it just seems like it was just, like kismet. That it was just meant to be. All those same people from back then, I still hang out with them pretty much. We all can't hang out like we used to, but we are all in touch!

JIM CHARLES: It was an outlet, a creative edge. I just didn't have any great aspirations. I was one of those that just didn't have that kind of direction. People would just say, "Hey! We need a guitarist!" and I'd join those bands! I would really like for people to understand that that song basically that whatever craft you have, if you do it with love you can do it right. That's the whole point! I always try to put a positive message in stuff when I do my own thing. And that's the best that I could do.

LARRY DUCKWORTH: That it was probably one of the most fun periods I've ever had in my life. Because it was such an adventure! And the fun competition! It's just one of those things where it all just happened. You experienced it and you were just sitting there worried about the next problem, the next tune. What might impress that chick the most, and it was all just a series of working through, and just the incredible friendship.

And the other thing that was just very different, in the Sixties, for me, was in that era with the music that was a huge amount of importance as far as what you believed. A school of thought, a style or fashion, and I know that's still here today, but then it put you in a clearly different camp from everyone else. Because you had the schism of the Vietnam War. And that huge political difference, because my dad was a businessman and very Republican, but music caused me to see things from a very different perspective, and to become a part of this other camp.

That is something that I think was unique in the Sixties, and is one of the reasons why we had this incredible blossoming of creativity that I don't think we see today. There's a lot of great music out there today, but you don't see breakthrough stuff like a Jimi Hendrix coming out and doing what he did. And that melding of styles and things that happened then that only playing for a cause, and some really good drugs, could produce.

DOUG JAMES: It was an exciting time, a very exciting time, and one of the subjects that

I now teach, a history of Rock Music course. Yeah, every summer I teach a history of Rock, and it's fascinating. Looking at it historically, and culturally. What a time! It is great for me, because I was there! I was in it and I was a part of it, and it gives me a great enthusiasm for the course material.

DAVID FLOYD: I realized that I could make money doing something that I loved, and would have done for free. And so, so what it did was it pretty much hooked me to playing music as a pretty easy life. So I took the easy way out and I never learned how to do anything else but play music.

BOB ROBINSON: To go out and play, and have the fun that we had, it was awesome. It eye-opening, and enlightening, and freeing, and it was just fun.

RANDY HALL: It was just the unbelievable enthusiasm and hope that we all had, that everything would be so much better. It was an international youth movement. You had bands coming out of England, Germany and all over the place, and we were all together on this thing. Then Jimi died, Janis died, Jim Morrison died. And some of us died. The music got more commercial. But for two, three years, it was incredible.

BARRY STACKS: I talked to a couple of guys that play our songs all the time in Australia. There's venues there that cater to garage-punk bands, and they play all the time. Where the hell were they when I needed them?

SHORTY NEHRENBERG: I think it was wonderful. It was just wonderful. Because it was all new experiences and new hopes. And boundless optimism. You felt like you could do anything. And that whatever it was that everyone was telling you couldn't do, you could do. Things were opening up to where the possibilities were endless, so to speak. There was a lot of enthusiasm, and not enough reality to understand that the right decisions are sometimes hard to make. The good and fun decisions are not necessarily the best decisions, so there were a lot of lessons to be learned. We were just completely optimistic.

BOBBY DONALDSON: I was really lucky to have grown up in the 1960s. The music that was coming out during that time, it was all getting a little deeper. More groove to it, more feeling. It makes me feel pretty good, that we're still playing. Especially the ones like Pat Walters, who can play anything. He's really good. There's also guys like Joe Orr, who was a little older than me. He was playing with Maurice Williams for years.

Joe and I had told lost touch, and one day I'm in the Miami airport, going up the escalator, and I hear, "Donaldson! What the hell are you doing here?" It was Joe. I love that these cats are still hitting it.

DAVE LONG: Things were changing. Before things got heavy, and drugs changed everything. Before we had to grow up. Back then, we had raging hormones, someone had had a guitar, and someone else had a driver's license.

STEVE STOECKEL: We grew up when the best music was being made. The music was what molded me.

PAT WALTERS: I'm totally proud of it, and glad to have experienced it first-hand actually in the Sixties. I played a lot of types of music over the years. It's been my life, and I don't know what else to do.

KEN KNIGHT: The Sixties were a great time to be apart of. To be 14, 15, 16 when the Beatles came out. I was kind of shy in school, and being in the Stowaways gave me confidence, and acceptance. And it got me a girlfriend that I married!

TIM TATUM: I think of the excitement of the moment, and playing a gig. The recognition of playing on stage. It was also very freeing. No politics, no economics, just pure music. It seems so long ago to me now, like it was in another life. But all in all, the memories were great.

DON TETREAULT: It was an era that won't be repeated. Everything was changing so fast. I'm not sure that I would want to go through the Sixties again, but you can see the results of what happened.

ROB THORNE: I'm still out there just playing like hell and having a big time! And I have no intention of retiring or quitting or stopping, as long as I can play! Somebody asked me a while back, "At what age do you stop playing drums?" And I said, " At what age do you stop breathing?"

DON DIXON: I want the same thing now, as then. Peace and love, and the chance to do one more song, one more show.

 Discography
Of Singles, Songs and LPs Discussed in This Book

45 RPM SINGLES

Abbreviations, "True Fine Lovin'," 1965.

Arrogance, "An Estimation"/"Black Death," Crescent City Records, 1969.

Bondsmen, "I See the Light"/"Our Time to Try," AMH Records, 1968.

Bondsmen, "Outasight"/"I Love You Yes I Do," Justice Records, 1968.

Bonnevilles, "Naughty Girl"/"Tell Me," Pyramid Records, 1966.

Challengers, "Moon Send My Baby"/"Dream," Kix International, 1970.

Changin' Tymes, "If You'll Love Me Again"/"Nobody," Hard Tymes, 1968.

Clear Blue Sky, "Morning of Creation"/"Ugly Girl," Romat Records, 1969.

Corsayers, "Change Your Ways"/"Cha Cha Cha Blues," JCP Records, 1965.

Counts IV, "Listen to Me"/"Lost Love," JCP Records, 1965.

Counts IV, "Spoonful"/"Where Are You," Date Records, 1966.

as **The Inexpensive Handmade Look**, "What Good Is Up"/"Ice Cream Man," Brunswick Records, 1968.

Cykle, "If You Can"/"In Love My Friend," Label 101, 1969.

Damascans, "Go Way Girl"/"Diane," Pyramid Records, 1966.

Dirte Floor (aka Centurions), with Willie Hobbs.

Willie Hobbs and the Dirte Floor, "Gloria"/"On the Move," Charay Records, 1969.

Willie Hobbs and the Dirte Floor, "Gloria"/"On the Move," Mercury Records, 1969.

Dukes, "It's Got the Whole World Shakin'," A Dukes Production, 1968.

18th Edition (New Mix), "Sundown"/"143rd Street," Panther Records, 1968.

Electric Love, "She Wants to Be Free"/"Dreaming of Her," Bandit Records, 1968.

Electric Love, "This Seat Is Saved"/"Gotta Get Back to My Baby," Charay Records, 1968.

Fabulous Plaids, "Let's Learn About Love"/"I'm Coming Home to You," Dixie Records, 1965.

Fabulous Wunz (aka The Wunz), "If I Cry"/"Please," Pyramid Records, 1967.

Grifs, "Catch a Ride"/"In My Life" 5D Records, 1965.

Grifs, "Keep Deaming"/"Northbound," Palmer Records, 1967.

Huckleberry Mudflap, "Blue Surf"/"Goodnight Mrs. Kollendoffer," Line 5 Records, 1969.

Shirley Hughey, "Pink and Green"/"When I Reach for You," Bandit Records, 1969.

Huns, "Shakedown"/"You Know," Pyramid Records, 1966.

IV Pak, "Boot-Leg"/"Whatzit?," Hippie Records, 1967.

Jesters, "Wrong Ticket"/"Happy," Golden Records, 1968.

King Bees, "Keep My Lovin'"/"I Want My Baby," Pyramid Records, 1966.

Londons, "You're the One"/"Old Man – A Thing of Age," Pyramid Records, 1968.

Marke V, "The Leader"/"Pay," JCP Records, 1966

Martians, "Martian Rock"/"Lawdy Miss Clawdy."

Mike & The Dimensions, "Little Latin Lupe Lu"/"Why," self-released, 1965.

Monarks, "I'm Gonna Be Glad"/"Gonna Miss Me Girl," Sound City Records, 1967.

Nightwalkers, "It'll Only Hurt for a Little While"/"Til There Was You," JCP Records, 1965.

Nomads, "Thoughts of a Madman," Tornado Records, 1967.

Nova Local, "If You Only Had the Time"/"Games," Decca Records, 1968.

Paragons, "Abba"/"Mister You're a Better Man Than I," Bobbi Records, 1966.

Psychotics, "I'm Determined"/"Still the Time Will Come," Uptown Records, 1967.

Psychotrons, "Death Is a Dream"/"Unchained Melody," BCP Records, 1969.

Revised Edition, "Thoughts of You"/"Illusions." Revise Records, 1969.

Rockets Combo, "Topless A-Go-Go"/"Summertime," Justice Records, 1966.

Ron-De-Voos, "A Trip So Wild"/"Run Run Run," Mastertone, 1967.

Sacred Irony, "I See Love," 1970.

Sands, "Mister You're a Better Man Than I," JCP Records, 1966.

Satyrs, "Don't Be Surprised"/ "Blue Blue World," Wal-Mor, 1966.

Scotsmen (Eastern N.C.), "Down and Out"/"A Groovy Place," Romat Records, 1967.

Si-Dells, "She's the Only Girl for Me"/"Watch Out Mother," East Coast Sound, 1968.

Speckulations, "Carol Carol," Justice Records, 1967.

Soul Twisters, "Swinging (On a Grape Vine)"/"Soul Fever." Romat Records, 1967.

Soul Twisters, "Doing Our Thing"/"If It Takes a Year," Romat Records, 1968.

Sound System, "Serenade"/"Take a Look at Yourself," Romat Records, 1969.

Sounds Unlimited, "Cool One"/"To Be in Love," Swal Records, 1967.

Symbols, "Can I See You Tonight?"/"Give Me Time," JCP Records, 1966.

Tamrons, "Wild Man"/"Stop Look Listen," Pyramid Records, 1967.

Teen-Beets, "I Guess That's Why You're Mine"/"Not in Love With Me," Chain Records, 1965.

Teen-Beets, "I Should Wait"/"Oh Baby," Chain Records, 1966.

as **The Beets**, "I Should Wait"/"Not in Love With Me," Dial Records, 1966.

as **Words of Luv**, "I'd Have to Be Outta My Mind"/"Tomorrow's a Long Time," Hickory Records, 1967.

Turks, "Fire"/"Adventure of Love," TK Records, 1968.

Tymes Syndicate Band, "An Uphill Climb"/"Change My Direction," ABC Records, 1968.

Unknown IV, "I Want You to Be Mine"/"All of the Time," JCP Records, 1965.

Unknown IV, "What's Gonna Happen"/"Give Me a Chance," JCP Records, 1966.

Vigilantes, "Ain't It Sad"/"Notice Me," JCP Records, 1966.

Virginians, "It's a Long Walk Back to Paradise"/"You Gotta Know (How To Love)," Epic Records, 1966.

Virginians, "A Piece of Cellophane"/"Looking Ahead," Epic Records, 1967.

as the **Good Earth**, "I Can See a Light/"A Funny Thing Happened (Anytime)," Dynovoice Records, 1968.

as the **Good Earth**, "Must I Really Go Thru This Again"/"There's More Than One Road to Philadelphia," Dynovoice Records, 1969.

as the **Good Earth Trio**, "How Deep Is the Ocean," Dynovoice Records, 1968.

photo by Daniel Coston

The New Mix self-titled album cover, 1968.

Young Ones, "Too Much Lovin'"/"Harbor Melon," Super Cool, 1966.

as **Psychic Motion**, "Big Teaser"/"It's You," Super-Cool Records, 1966.

ALBUMS

Bonnevilles, *Bringing It Home*, Justice Records, 1966.

Cykle, self-titled album, 1969. (Reissued on CD with Young Ones/Psychic Motion tracks as **Cykle Presents**: The Young Ones.")

Dirte Floor, *Funky Soul*, Charay Records, 1968.

Doug Clark and the Hot Nuts, *Nuts to You*, Gross Records, 1961

Generations Combo, *Meet the …*, Justice Records, 1967.

Horde, *Press Buttons Firmly*, self-released, 1968. (Reissued in 2013 through Break-A-Way Records.)

collection of Daniel Coston
The Nova Local "Nova 1" album cover, 1968.

Kallabash Corp., self-titled LP, Uncle Bill, 1970.

New Mix, self-titled, United Artists, 1968.

Nightriders, *Introducing*, Justice Records, 1967.

Nova Local, *Nova 1*, Decca Records, 1968.

Speculations, *Walking the Dog in the Midnight Hour*, Justice Records, 1966.

Starliters, *Journey With the Starliters*, Justice Records, 1966.

Stowaways, *In Our Time*, Justice Records, 1967. (Now available through Collectible Records.)

Varcels, *Hang Loose*, Justice Records, 1967.

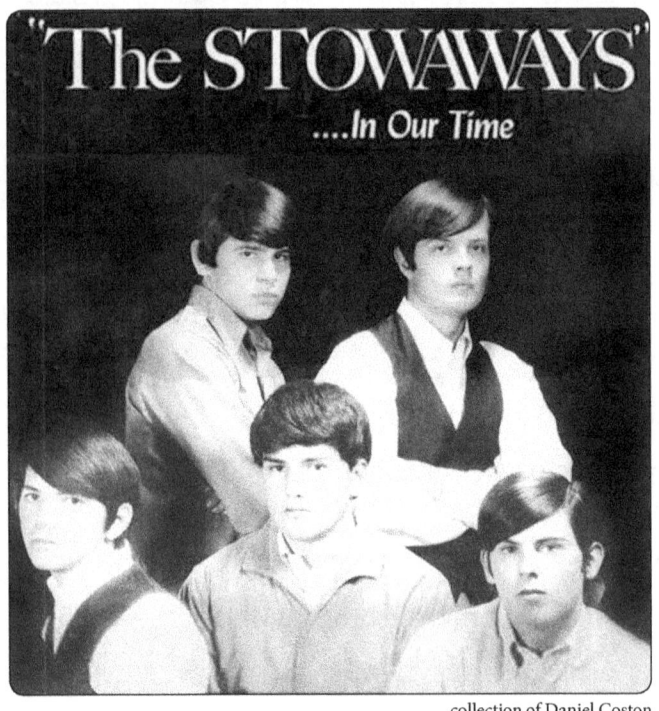
collection of Daniel Coston
The Stowaways "In Our Time" album cover, 1967.

INDEX

A

5 Royales..3
18th Edition................91, 92, 93, 110
36 Bandstand.............................109
A.L. Brown High School................84
A&R Talent...................................37
ABC Records................................76
AMG Records...............................30
AMH...121
"Abba"...............41, 42, 44, 46, 49, 50,
       51, 52, 53, 54, 83, 84, 87, 150, 151
Abbadons..22, 23, 45, 46, 52, 53, 54, 62, 86, 87
Abbey Road................................125
Abernethy, Rod...........................126
Ahramoonie, George.....................61
"Ain't No Telling".........................138
Ajents..39
Alairlura.....................................133
Alamo..47
Albritton, Boyd..............16, 24, 85, 130
Alexander, Arthur..........................23
Alexander, Mark............................12
Alexander Graham..................62, 99
Alexander Graham Junior High..62, 111, 134
Allen, Ken...................................123
Allman Brothers..........................146
Allman Joys................................138
Aloha Club..................................117
Altamont....................................129
Am Vets...8
Amboy Dukes..........................32, 63
Amboy Lounge.............................69
American Bandstand...................110
An Uphill Climb............................76

Andrews, Dickie..........................117
Animals................19, 40, 88, 108
"Anna"...23
Appalachian State University....38, 68
Aqualads......................................85
Arhooly......................................144
Arrogance..................................126
Arthur Lee and Love.....................42
Arthur Smith Studios..3, 36, 49, 70, 74, 75, 129
Asheville Recreation Park..............69
Atlanta Pop Festival....................139

B

The B&G Trading Post....................7
BMI...52
Baby's in Black.............................16
Baker, Danny..............................146
Bandit..................................72, 135
Bar-Kays......................................88
Barbour, Gene.............................11
Barker, Gary.................................92
Barker, Johnny........................91, 92
Barkley, John (Johnny).....40, 41, 68, 95, 96,
                                           129, 150
Barons.........25, 26, 27, 47, 48, 58, 87, 88
Baxley, Ronnie............................122
Beach Boys..................10, 35, 36, 117
The Beach Party...........................76
Beatle Juniors..............................25
Beatles.......3, 13, 15, 16, 17, 18, 19, 20, 21,
       23, 29, 32, 38, 40, 45, 63, 64, 78, 82, 83, 89,
       90, 91, 92, 106, 108, 109, 116, 124, 149, 155
Beau Brummels.....................24, 106
Beaver, Joe..................................93
Bedpost Reunion........................117

Bee Bumble & The Stingers 71	Botniks 94
Bee Gees 88, 129	Bowen, Jim 120
Belk 111	The Box 38
Bell, Dave 111	Brother Ross The Boss 111
Belmont Abbey 141	Brakefield, Dave. 20
Belmont Senior High School. 33	Brakefield, David 27, 38
"Bend Me Shape Me" 128	Branch, Roger 129
Bennett, Tony. 112	Break-A-Way Records 119
Benton, Johnny 62	Breem, Biff 117
Berger, Jacob v	Brentson, Jackie 2
Berger, Jake . . . . iv, 1, 13, 14, 16, 22, 25, 27, 28, 32, 34, 38, 42, 48, 53, 55, 57, 58, 59, 60, 61, 62, 81, 83, 84, 85, 86, 89, 96, 97, 98, 100, 106, 122, 128, 130, 134, 137, 138, 139, 141, 144, 146, 147, 149, 150, 151, 152	Briarhopper, Homer 121
	Briarhoppers 1
	Bridges, Alicia 148
	Britt, Billy 121
	Britt, Dickie 122
	Britton, Mike v
Berry, Chuck 124	Brodie, Diane 148
"Big Teaser" 123	Brodie's Down Home Cooking 148
Big WAYS Battle of the Bands 41, 129	Brooke Records 3
The Big Picture 102	Brown, David 91, 92, 93, 145, 146
Bigham, Henry 84	Brown, Gaines 53, 86
Birdland 69	Brown, Gene 68
Bishop, Chris v	Brown, George 111
Black Death 126	Brown, James 3, 11, 30, 32, 37, 59, 61, 66, 109, 120
Black Sabbath 125	
Bland, Bobby "Blue" 116	Brown, Les 5, 93
"Blue Blue World" 69	Brown, Nappy 2, 3
Blue Note Lounge 10	Brown, Tate 59
"Blue Surf" 123	Brown, West Side James 109
Bluenotes 3	Brown Derby 69
Blues Magoos 109	Brown Eyed Girl 82
The Bob Ledford Show 72	Buckinghams 32, 51, 63
Bolick, John 20	Buffalo Springfield 88
Bondsmen 119, 120	Burdon, Eric 40
Booger Band 137	Burgess, Gerald 86
Booker T. & The MG's 17	Burroughs, William 118
Boot-Leg 77	Burton, James 4
Born In Chicago 87	Bush, Laura 83
Borthwick, Robin 79, 80	

Butterfield Blues Band 87
Byrds 24, 36

C

CBS 122
CIA 145
CKLU 30
Cabbage, River 119
Camp Thunderbird 86
Campbell, Glen 106
Canned Heat 141
Capitol 15, 36, 37
Capitol Records 15, 36
Capps, Jimmy 122
Captain Speed and
His Fungi Electric Mothers 79
Carolina Theater 7
Carolinas Rock & Roll Rememberd v
Carpenter, Pat 82
Carrigan, Dickie 40, 150
Casa Loma 69
Cash, Johnny 2
Cashman, Barbara "Bobbie" 49, 50, 52
Cast 88
Catalinas 6, 7, 10, 11, 12, 29, 38, 57,
59, 91, 92, 109, 110, 115, 137
Catawba College 73
"Catch A Ride" 21, 29, 30, 32, 53, 90, 150
Cato, Jennifer 100
Cavaliers 11, 111, 125
Cave 68
Cavern 151
The Celestial Omnibus 117
Cellar 63, 91, 137, 138, 145
The Cellar 91
Center Theatre 10
Centurions 71
Chad & Jeremy 19, 118

Chambers, Mac 79
"Change My Direction" 76
"Change Your Ways" 116
Changin' Tymes 76
Chapparrals 36
Charles, Bill 42, 43, 44, 52
Charles, Jim 42, 43, 44, 45, 46, 47, 48,
51, 52, 53, 54, 63, 153
Charles, Ray 2, 108
Charlotte Coliseum . . 7, 31, 47, 63, 67, 84, 125
Charlotte Women's Club 128
Charlottetown 45
Checkmates 120
Chess Records 2
Chesterfields 120
Christ Episcopal Church 28
Christie, Lou 66
Chronosynclasticindibulum 149
Chronosynclasticinfindibulum 138
Cibo House Pizza 35
Civic Center 70, 71
Clapton, Eric 24, 57, 84
Clark, Dave 19, 30, 88
Clark, Dick 66, 76
Clark, Manny 29, 30, 50, 53
"Clear Blue Sky" 123
Clique 78
Cobras 122
Cochrane Junior High 25, 46
Cohen, Melvin 24, 55, 95, 129, 137, 138,
147, 151
Cole, Clay 112
Coliseum (Charlotte) 7, 31, 47, 63, 66, 67,
84, 98, 125
Collectibles 150
Collins, Mojo 122
Collins, Paul 117
Columbia Studios 118

Combat! 106
Conley, Arthur. 61
Corsayors 116
Coston, Daniel . . iv, v, 1, 3, 7, 8, 10, 11, 13, 15, 19, 23, 24, 25, 28, 29, 31, 33, 35, 36, 39, 40, 41, 42, 44, 45, 46, 47, 48, 49, 50, 51, 52, 54, 55, 59, 61, 65, 68, 69, 71, 73, 74, 76, 78, 79, 80, 82, 83, 88, 90, 91, 94, 95, 97, 107, 108, 109, 110, 111, 112, 113, 114, 115, 116, 117, 119, 120, 121, 122, 124, 125, 126, 127, 129, 130, 131, 133, 135, 137, 139, 140, 144, 145, 146, 148, 149, 150, 151, 152
Counts IV. 122
Covay, Don. 17
Crawford, Bob 16, 21, 101
Cream 17, 59, 99, 134
Crescendos. 117
The Crested T. 28
Crewe, Bob. 115
Cross, Don 111
"Crossroads" 83
"Crystal Ship". 63
Cummings, Burton. 63
Cykle. 123

D

DAR Constitution Hall 62
Dale, Dick. 10
Damascans. 75, 76
Date Records 122
Dave Clark Five. 19, 30
Davidson College 141
Davies, Dave. 62
Davis, Cliff 53, 145
Davis, Spencer. 134
Davison, Scott 126
Day, Bill. 120
The Daybreak Show 121
Deal, Harry. 11, 72

Deans, Hubert 119, 120
Decca. 115, 118, 129
Decca Records 118
December's Children 40
Deliverance 3
Deltas 6
Diamonds. 3
Diddley, Bo. 6
Dick Clark Shower of Stars 66
Die Hards 35, 42, 82, 83, 109
Dinelli, Dino 122
Dion, Celine. 149
Dirte Floor 71
Dixie Dregs 57
Dixon, Dicky 7
Dixon, Don 122, 124, 125, 126, 127, 155
Dobbins, Debby. 51, 52, 63, 83, 91, 99, 136, 145, 153
Dodson, Ed 80
"Don't Be Angry" 2
"Don't Be Surprised". 69
Donaldson, Bobby 5, 16, 19, 23, 24, 37, 38, 61, 62, 65, 84, 85, 98, 99, 111, 130, 148, 154
Donovan. 67
Doo, Dickie 111
Doors 82
Dorton Arena 121
Dotson, Ed 135
Double Door Inn. . . . . iv, 138, 144, 146, 149
Doug Clark and the Hot Nuts 115, 125
Douglas, Ben 5
Douglas, Bob 5
Douglas Furs 5
Dragon's Breath 33
Dragon's Foot. 33
Dragon's Lair 33
Drake, Tom 147

"Keep Dreaming" 90
Drifters 120
The Drum. 99
"Dueling Banjos" 3
Duckworth, Jimmy 18, 45, 53, 98, 130,
134, 145, 151
Duckworth, Joe 63
Duckworth, Larry 18, 46, 53, 86, 130,
131, 151, 153
Dugo, Mike v
Dukes 32, 63, 119, 120, 121
Dukes of Durham 120, 121
Durations 83, 128
Durham High School 121
Dylan, Bob 24
Dynovoice 115

E

Eagles 144
Earnhardt, "Big Al" .97
East Coast Sound .119
Easter, Mitch 78, 79, 80
Eastway 20, 26, 48, 51, 128
Eastway Junior High 20, 128
Eatmon, Chuck 123
Eckerd's 98
Ed Sullivan (TV show) 13, 15, 16, 78, 122
Edwards, Dennis 9, 36, 60, 74, 87, 88,
89, 101, 105, 133, 139, 144
Efird, Dave 11
El Morocco Supper Club 10
Elks Club 5, 8
Embers 11, 12, 115
End Zone 145
Epic 115, 116
Epic Records 116
Epstein, Brian .15, 134
Eradicators 75, 78
Eros 145
Ernie's Hi-Fi and Camera 59
Ernie's Records 9, 59
Ernie's Records Shop 9
Everly Brothers 106
Excels 109

F

FBI 145
Fabian 66
Fabulous Corsairs .116
Fabulous Wunz 70
Falkenberry, Mike .109
Fallows, Robert 23
Fantastik Four 75
Little Feat 67
Federal, Lenny 144, 149
Fellows, Danny "Munk" 24, 48, 145
Ferreri, Ernie 4, 147
Fields, Toni 75
Fillmore 67
Famous Flames 30
Festival In The Park 22, 23, 56, 57, 86
First Edition 93
Five Americans 121
Flamingo Drive-In .78
Flares 90, 146, 148
Fletcher, Donny . . 4, 21, 33, 34, 63, 82, 94, 140
Floretta Baylin's Dance Academy 79
Floyd, David 5, 18, 34, 35, 57, 58, 90,
146, 148, 149, 154
Folkways Magazine .9
"For Your Love" 20
Forest Theater 121
Four Tops 65
Fox, Charlie 118
Fox, John 30, 32
Foxhole 144
Fragmentary Blue .89

Frank's Pawn Shop 58
Frankie & The Damons 123
Freddy and the Dreamers 19
Freed, Alan. 2
Freedom Park 22, 45, 87, 138, 139
Freshmen, Four 8
Friedman, Ken. . . . . .v, 72, 121, 124
Frieze, Carla. 139
Ft. Bragg 103, 104
Fuller, Don 117
"Funky Soul" 71

G

Gail, Jack. 110
Galaxie III Studios 72
Galaxies. 6, 11, 21
Galligan, Gene. 120
Garinger High School . . 33, 48, 51, 89, 99, 132
Garner, Tommy. 91, 92
Garrett, Jack. v
Gauchos 106
Gaye, Marvin 17
Gayelord 34
The Gayelords 33, 34, 90
Geller, Arnie. 30
Generations Combo 74
Genesis 136
"Genie" 75
The Gentleman Bandit 135
Gentry, Bobby 82
Gentry House 59
George, Lowell. 67
Gerry and the Pacemakers. 19
"Girl Watcher" 11
Give Us A Break 126
Glasgow, Jimmy. 14, 126
"Gloria" 33, 39, 89, 108
Glory Cykle 123

"Go Way Girl" 75
Good Bad And The Ugly (GBU) 56, 92, 136, 137, 140, 147
Good Earth 115
"Good Lovin'" 108
Good Time People, Inc. 93
Gooding, Ray. 111
Grand Funk Railroad 149
Granny Goes Grooving 110
Grass Roots 82
Green, Mike. 111
Green Dragon 75
Greer, Mike 125
Greystones 23, 61
Griffin, Neil 57
Griffith, Andy 3
Grifs. 29, 31, 32, 35, 90, 91, 150
Gross Records 115
Guess Who. 63
"Guitar Boogie" 3
Guthrie, Woody. 116

H

Hall, Randy . . . 28, 49, 134, 137, 138, 147, 154
Hall, Ted 26
Hamilton, George IV 3
Hammond, John 9
"I Wanna Hold Your Hand" 18, 51, 91
Handy, Wayne 3
Happening 76, 119
Happening '69 119
The Happenings 118
Harding High School 64
Harris Teeter 100
Harry Deal and the Galaxies. 11
Hawthorne Junior High 84
Hawthorne Recreation Center 107
Hector 137

Herman's Hermits 19, 27, 30, 48, 63, 84
A Hard Day's Night. 78
Hardin, Jeff. 123
Harding, Barbara. 111
Harris, Bernie 76
Harrison, Wilbert 3
Hatcher, George. 71
Hawkins, Charley 128
Hayberg, Mary Ann 8
Hayden, Tim 68
Hayes, Johnny 122
Haywood, Ken. 120
Head, Larry 8
Hendrix, Jimi 17, 23, 24, 61, 63, 68, 79,
85, 89, 99, 125, 138, 139, 153
Heptigue, Bill. 54
Herbert, Steve 126
Herman's Hermits 19, 27, 30, 48, 63, 84
"Hey Joe" 109
Hickory Records 74
Hideaway 69
High Fidelity Sales 69
Highlanders 69
Hinkle, Bob 68, 69, 71, 115
Hinson, Unknown 146
Hippie Hill 139
Hippie Records 78
Hirt, Al 125
Hit Attractions. 26
The Hit Parader 106
Hobbs, Willie. 71
Hodads 34, 35, 36
Hodge, Russell 3, 109
Holland, Eddie. 71
Hollies. 30, 63, 84
Holmes, Jackie 76
Holsapple, Peter. 78
"Honky Tonk Women" 151
Hoover, Jamie 146
Hope For Happiness. 79
Horde 119
Hostetler, John. 117
Hostetler, Johnny. 138
Hot-Cha 62
"Hot Nuts" 115, 125
House Of Pancakes. 97
House Of Sound Studios 77
"House Of The Rising Sun" 39, 42, 47
Howlin' Wolf 2
Howren 25, 45
Howren's. 45
Huckleberry Mudflap 123
Hughey, Shirley 72
Hullabaloo 106
Hullabaloos 106
Hummingbird 145
Huns 75
Huntley, Danny . . . 45, 49, 51, 52, 84, 110, 130
Hyman, Buddy. 75

I

IV Pak. 77, 78
"I Don't Know What It Is" 3
"I Guess That's Why You're Mine" 74
"I See Love" 78
"I See The Light" 121
"I Want To Hold Your Hand" 15
"I'd Have To Be Outta My Mind" 75
"I'm A Man" 27
"If I Cry" 70
"If You Only Had The Time" 118
Ike & Tina Turner 116
"Illusions Of You" 76
Imperturbable Teutonic Griffin 79
Impressions 19
"In My Own Time" 129

Inexpensive Handmade Look 122
"Incense and Peppermints" 79
Irwin Building 47
"It Won't Be Wrong" 36
"It's You" 123

J

JCP. 116, 122, 123
J. Frank Wilson and the Cavaliers 111
Jackson, Jesse 133
Jade East 120
Jagger, Mick 63
Jaguars 6
Jamerson, James 65
James, Doug 4, 5, 16, 18, 27, 38, 39, 85, 131, 147, 153
James, Elmore 1
Jan & Dean 10
Jarvi, Karl 27, 38, 92, 145
Java 125
Jay & The Techniques 71
Jays, Vee 78
Jeremiah 145
Jesters 122, 124
Joe's A Go Go 28, 128
John Hardee Shoes 60
Johnny B. Goode 109
Jones, Brian 143
Jones, George 16
Jones, Mel 117
Joplin, Janis 65
Jules Verne 130
Justice Records 73, 74, 150
Justus, Theresa 72

K

Kaleidoscope Productions 138
Kallabash Corporation 76
Kaplan, Stan 148

Kay, John 114
Kenny Rogers and the Key Club 95
Kilgo, Jimmy 94, 107, 110, 141
Kilgo's Canteen . . . 52, 106, 107, 108, 109, 110
King, Alan 31, 36
King, B.B. 1
King, Ben E. 3, 62
King, Martin Luther Jr. 133
King Bees 75
Kingsmen 124
Kinks 16, 19, 24, 30, 32, 62, 63, 106
Kirby, Fred 1, 4, 24
Kirkland, Robert 125
Knight, Ken . . 20, 21, 36, 37, 74, 94, 101, 150, 155
Knollwood (Church) Coffeehouse 80
Knowles, Tommy 119
Kustoms 123

L

Lambeth, Phil 117, 118
Larry's Sound Department 87, 130
Lassiter, Henry 62
"Last Date" 111
Lavoie, Jeanne 110
"The Leader" 123
Led Zeppelin 79, 106, 140
Led Zeppelin I 79
Lee, Phil . . . . v, 119, 120, 121, 122, 150
Lee, Purvis 131
Lee Edwards High School 69, 70, 71
Leeper, Chatty Hattie 110, 111
Lennon, John 15
Pace, Leroy 48
Les Brown's Big Band 5
"Let's Live For Today" 82
Levasseur, Bill 117
Lewis., J. D. 119

Lewis, Jerry Lee 2
Life Magazine. 16
"Light My Fire" 82, 95, 111
"Like A Rolling Stone" 24
Lily Whyte Lyres 44
Lindsay, Mark 38, 119
Lindsey, Jim 25, 27
Lipscomb, Vic 116
"Listen To Me" 122
"Little Black Egg" 33
"Little Darlin'" 3
"Little Latin Lupe Lu" 122
"Little Red Rooster" 16
Little Richard 17, 18, 66
Lloyd Thaxton 106
The Lloyd Thaxton Show 106
Loafers 7
Locke, Cindy 100
The Lodge. 10
Loflen, Ronnie 144
Loftin, Karen 100
Londons 75, 124
Long, Dave (David) 8, 16, 28, 40, 50,
57, 86, 96, 141, 155
"Long Walk Back To Paradise" 116
Looking Glass 72
Loose Screws 108
"Lost Love" 122
"Louie Louie" 39
Lounge, Riverboat. 69
Love, Electric 72
Lovin' Spoonful 62, 122
"Love Me Do" 17
"Love Potion #9" 22
Love Valley 146, 147
Love Valley Festival. 146
Lovin' Spoonful 62
Lowe, Phil 27, 87, 88, 140, 145

Lowery, Willie 124
The Loyal Opposition. 79, 80
Lumbee, NC 124
Luved Ones 118

m

MGM 30
Magazine, Mountain Xpress v
"Mr. Tambourine Man" 22
Magucci Bowling Team 116
Manhattans 112
Manson, Charles 81
Margolin, Bob 144
Marke 5. 123
Marke V Studios 70
Martians 77
Martin, Colin 68
Mattox, Johnny 99
May, Elmon 128
Mayfield, Curtis. 19
McAuliff, Sharon. 100
McCartney, Paul 145
McFayden. 57, 58
McFayden's. 58
McGlohon, Loonis 125
McLeod, Zan 4, 24, 48, 56, 57, 82, 83,
84, 98, 101, 109, 129, 131, 136, 145, 147, 152
McMillan, Corky. 80
McPhatter, Clyde. 3
Meet The Beatles 116, 124
Mellons. 59
Melvin The Grocery Boy 111
Memorial Staium, ... 48, 84
Mendyk, Joe. 119
Mental Health Clinic 102
Mercury 11, 71, 115
Mercury Records. 71
Meyer, Bob 11

Miami Pop Festival 135
Mickey's Lounge 7
Midnight Hour 120
Midnight Sun. 138
Midwood Elementary School 20
Mike & The Dimensions 122
Miles, Buddy 24
Milestone 138
Mills, Billy 71
Minority 117
Misfits 71
"Mister, You're A Better Man Than I" . .49, 84
Mitchell, Woody 144
Moby Grape. 97
Modulation Blooze Band. 36, 87, 88, 133
Monarks 123
Monkees 63, 82
"Moon River". 47
Moore, Tim 47, 48, 51, 100, 137, 145, 150
Moose 8
Morgan, J.W. 111
Morris, Nelson. 25, 27
Morrison, Van 82
Morse, Steve 57
Moss, John 8
Moss, Sam 78, 79
Mothers of Invention 67
Motley Jesters. 122
Move 23, 79
Mr. College Guy 18
Mr. Glasspak and His Magic Mufflers 79
Mr. Hi Style 38, 59, 60
Muir, Doug. 79
Mullis, Helen 100
Mullis, Jon 8, 57, 145, 149
Mump. 32
"Murder In My Heart For The Judge" 97
Music Incorporated 5
"My Little Red Book" 42
Myers, Mark. 4, 40, 41
Myers Park 28, 33, 85, 105, 111
Myers Park Methodist 28
Mynd Garden. 140

n

Naples, David. 75
Naples, Toni 76
Nature Museum. 22, 45
Nehrenberg, Sally vi
Nehrenberg, Shorty. . .9, 32, 35, 36, 58, 59, 62,
   63, 67, 88, 103, 104, 105, 133, 134, 139, 154
Nehrenburg, Shorty 89, 144
Nelson, Ricky. 4
New Establishment. 126
New Mix. 91, 92, 93, 110, 138, 145
New York City Records 59
"New York Mining Disaster 1941" 88
Newberg's Mr. Hi Style. 59, 60
Newcomers. 125
Newport Folk Festival 24
Newton, Calvin 73
Nicky's. 10
"The Night Time Is The Right Time" 2
Nighthawks 144
Nightriders. 74
Nightwalkers 123
Noblemen. 85, 86
Nomads. 77, 117
Noone, Peter 63
North Carolina Symphony 125
North Mecklenburg High School. 39
"Northbound" 90
Northern High School 120
"Not In Love With Me" 74
Nova 1. 118
Nova Express 118

Noval Local 117
The Nova Local 117, 118
Nuremberg, Shorty 87
Nuts To You 115

O

The O'Kaysions 11
Oakley, Steve 116
"Ode To Billy Joe" 82
Olympic 83
"Open Window" 127
Opton, Jim 117
Orbison, Roy 2
Orr, Joe 154
Osser, Abe 93
Osser, Glenn 93
"Open Window" 127
"Our Time To Try" 122
Orange Purple Marmalade 72
Owens, Buck 149
Ozark 69

P

Pace, Bobby 45, 52, 99, 140, 151
Pace, Johnny 46, 48, 50, 52, 110, 146
Pagans 46
Page, Jimmy 106
Page, Kim 117
Panther Records 92, 93
"Papa's Got A Brand New Bag" 3
Paragons 28, 35, 38, 41, 42, 45, 46, 47,
    48, 49, 50, 51, 52, 53, 54, 55, 58, 83, 84, 86,
    87, 88, 89, 110, 115, 117, 130, 138, 140, 151
Park Center . 7, 11, 19, 21, 36, 65, 66, 84, 112,
    141
Park Road 22, 35, 49, 56, 59, 84, 98
Park Road Shopping Center 22, 35, 56,
    59, 84, 98
Partis, Danny 46

Paul Revere & The Raiders 38, 71, 119
Paul, Willie 62
Paul's Lounge 7, 131, 138
Pavillion, Asheville 69, 80
The Pavilion 80, 110
"Pay" 51, 123
Payges, Yellow 80
Payne, David 62
Pearson, Philip 119, 122
Penetrations 84
Pennington, Jack 8
"Penny Lane" 82
Perkins, Carl 2
Peter & Gordon 19, 124
Phantom Raiders 75
Phantasmagoria 113, 135, 136, 137, 147
Phillips, Ronnie 18, 40, 95, 129, 150
Phillips, Sam 2
Pic And Bill 71
Pickens, Charles 68, 71
Pickett, Wilson 17
Royal Pines 68, 69
"Pink And Green" 72
Pitney, Gene 107
Pitt Records 123
Pitt Sound Studios 123
Plant And See 124
Platters 117
Plavidal, Gary 27, 39, 134
"Please" 70
Poe, Buck 120
Pollock, Vance v
Pop, Grady 123
Pope, Scott 76
Pope, Tom 35, 41, 109, 124, 152
Potts, Genial Gene 111
Pour Souls 124
Premiers 130

Presley, Elvis 2, 7, 8, 10, 17, 44, 116
Presley, Larry 138
Pretty Things 25, 27
Procol Harum 82, 141
Prolepsis 126
Pruitt, Bob 72
Psychic Motion 123
Psychotrons 123
"Purple Haze" 62, 63, 111
Purple Onion 33
Purple Penguin 40, 41, 83, 137, 138
"The Pusher" 114
Pyramid Records 70, 75

Q

Quigley, Larry .99, 100

R

RF Studios 93
"The Race Is On" 16
The Racquets 125
Radio Ethiopia 113
Ram 145
Randolph Junior High 135
Raper, Mike 41, 95, 150
Rascals 108, 122
"Raunchy" 3
Raven Records 78
Ravens 64, 65, 75
"Reach Out (I'll Be There)" 38, 129
Reactions 122
Rebel Lounge 37
Record Bar 119
Red, White, and Defiantly Blues Band 134
Red Worms 142
Redding, Otis 17, 128
Reid, Terry 146
Reliable Music 25, 55, 56, 57, 58
Reliable Pawn & Loan 55
Reliable Pawn Shop 25, 58
Renown Records 3
"Repent Walpurgis" 141
Reverbs 123
Revised Edition 76
Reynolds, Bill 128
Rhythm Kings 2
Rich, Buddy 12
Rich, Sam 121
Richards, Keith 113
Riffin v
Rigby, Will 78
Rivieras 7, 11, 12
Road Band 122
Robbins, Guy 35, 36
Roberts, Bill 134
Robinson, Bob 40, 62, 95, 111, 129, 154
Robinson, Eric 101, 137, 138, 146
"Rocket 88" 2
Rockets Combo 75
Rolling Stone Magazine 24, 67, 106
Rolling Stones 18, 19, 23, 27, 31, 106,
112, 134, 143, 151
Rollins, Billy 93
Romat 123
Ron-De-Voos 71
Rorem, Ned 125
Roulettes 68, 69
Royal Roulettes 68
Royal Shades 71
Rumors 126
Russell, Leon 106
Ryder, Mitch 116

S

Sacred Irony .77, 78, 80
Salvation 137, 138, 145

Sam & Dave 137	Shindig 106
Sam and Dave 120	Shirelles............................117
Sam the Sham & The Pharoahs........16, 71	Shreed Holding Company..............138
Samples, Mary Ann 82	Si-Dells 119, 120
Sands................................124	Silver, Long John....................111
Sands Of Time........................ 117	Sinclairs.........................19, 20, 27
Santa, John.....................120, 122	Skinner, Roy................. 21, 91, 101
Satans 35	Sky Club 69
"Satisfaction" 29, 58	Small Faces......................82, 134
Satrurday Night Country Style 3	Smash Mercury 11
Satyrs.............................69, 70	Smith, Arthur 3, 4, 30, 36, 49, 70, 74,
Schifman, Sammy......................62	75, 109, 129
Schinan, Cam........................116	Smith, Brad 14
Schinhan, Cam 119	Smith, Chuck Dale 78
Scofield, Tim 68	Smith, Dale......................78, 80
Scotsmen 32, 33, 35, 123	Smith, Dean 116
Scott, Billy..........................11	Smith, Junior 147
Scott, Charlie 116	Smith, Lanny 75
Screws........................107, 108	Smith, Mike 134
Searchers...........................19	Smith, Ronnie 25, 27, 38, 39
Sebastian, John 62	Smith, Tommy.......................37
Sedgfield Junior High...............46, 53	"Smokestack Lightning"................87
Seeger, Pete........................116	Soft Machine 79
Seiwell, Denny......................145	Sonny and the Sunliners 11
Senior, Tony 97	Sossamon, Jimmy 122, 123
Sgt. Pepper's Lonely Hearts Club Band 82	"Soul Finger" 88
Shackles 117	Soul Inc............................62
Shadows 65, 118	Soul Twisters 123, 124
The Shadows 65, 118	Sound City Studios...................123
Shadyz 71	The Sound System...................123
"Shake A Tail Feather" 54	Sounds Unlimited....................75
"Shakedown" 75	South 29 Bowling Lanes................47
Shaw, Ogie 126	South Meck 33, 89, 105
Shazam 79	Spare Change......................138
She's About A Mover 120	Sparrow, Don........................117
Shepherd, Andy....................115	Sparrow, Kathy.....................142
Sherman, Bobby 80	Speculations.....................74, 75
Sherwood Forest.....................63	Spectaculars 122

Speed Limit 35 137
Spinosa, Dave. 145
Spongetones. 38, 146, 149
Spontanes. 11
Sprinkle, Larry . . 110, 112, 113, 114, 138, 148
Spyder Web 28, 33
St. Martin's 39
Stacks, Barry 6, 11, 16, 21, 29, 31, 32,
                   63, 90, 91, 130, 150, 154
Stallion Club 120
Stamey, Chris. .78, 79
"Stand By Me" 62
Standing in the Shadows of Motown 65
Starliters 74
Statesville National Guard Armory 84
"Stay" 3
Steele, Henry 92, 140, 145
Steppenwolf 114
Stevens, Ralph 123
Stewart, Billy 66
Stewart, Lee 8
Stoeckel, Steve 17, 20, 37, 38, 51, 56,
                   82, 100, 111, 145, 155
Stones 16, 17, 18, 19, 23, 25, 27,
             29, 30, 31, 32, 38, 63, 82, 89, 106, 112,
             113, 134, 143, 149, 151
"Stop Look Listen". 75
Stout, Marty 126
Stowaways 36, 73, 74, 94, 129, 150, 155
Straggle Inn 28, 35
Stravakis, Nick. 8
Strawberry Fields 82
Streisand, Barbara. 112
"Suddenly" 126
Sugarcreek 140
Sullivan, Ed 13, 15, 16, 78, 122
"Summertime". 120
Sun Studios. 2

Sunliners. 11
"Sunshine Of Your Love" 111
Surfmates 75
Sustar's Music. 25, 59
Sustar's Music Store. 25
Swafford, Bill 115
Swan Silvertones 116
The Sweetcorn Serenade 68
Swinging Sensations 75
Symbols. 123

T

T.C. Atlantic. 27, 37, 38
Tamrons 75
Tams 17, 137
Tanner's. 8, 56
Tassels 11
Tatum, Tim 20, 36, 37, 73, 74, 94, 95,
                   100, 129, 150, 155
Taxmen. 123
Taylor, Alex 116
Taylor, Hugh 116, 117
Taylor, Isaac 116
Taylor, James 116, 125
Taylor, Livingston 116, 117
Teen-Beats 74
Teen Cotillion 128
Teen Screen 123
Teenage Frolics 119
Temptations 17, 24, 65, 112, 114, 131
Tetreault, Don 28, 29, 63, 100, 134,
                   139, 147, 155
Tex, Joe 120
Thomas, Archie. 120, 122
Thomas Wolfe Auditorium 70
Thorne, Rob. 5, 6, 7, 8, 10, 11, 17, 29,
           38, 59, 65, 91, 103, 109, 110, 126, 137, 138,
           145, 148, 155
Thornton, Jim 3

"Thoughts" 76
Tides 120
Tillman, Don 34, 35
Tillman's Music 25, 45, 57, 58
Tillotson, Johnny 107
"Time Won't Let Me" 109
The Tin Can 28
Tobacco A Go-Go Volume 1 121
Tobacco A Go-Go Volume 2 124
Tobacco A Go-Go Volume 3 72
"Tobacco Road" 62, 63
"Tommorow's A Long Time" 75
Tommy James & The Shondells 70, 71
"Too Much Lovin'" 123
Townhouse Three 115
The Tree House 7
Treehouse 138
Trick 147
"A Trip So Wild" 71
Trinity Church 28
Trojans 31
Turner, Ike 2
Turks 77, 124
Turner, Randy 53
Turtles 124
"Tutti Fruiti" 66
Twi-lighters 22
"Twist and Shout" 20
Twitty, Conway 112
Tymes Syndicate Band 76

U
UNCC 75
Ultimate Spinach 67
Uncle Bill 76
United Artists Records 11, 91
Unterberger, Richie v

V
VI Pack 77, 78
Vaden, Charles 62
Valentine, Leslie 100
Vanderlip, Gill 4, 51, 107, 108
Varcels 74
Variations 74
Ventures 18
Veteran's Park 100
Via, Skip 117
Vietnam War 97, 98, 101, 102, 103, 104,
              105, 126, 129, 144, 145, 150, 153
Vigilantes 124
Village Square 109, 110
Villagers 110, 138, 140
Virginians 115, 116
Vogues 117

W
WAIR 78
WAYS .. 16, 32, 34, 41, 95, 110, 111, 114, 116,
                                    129, 148
WBT 107
WBTV 109, 110, 125, 145
WCNC 109, 148
WGBR 122
WGIV 29, 30, 32, 50, 51, 110, 111
WISE 70
WIST 16, 30, 32, 36, 111, 112, 113, 114
WIST Battle Of The Bands 36
WKIX 116, 119
WKSY 68
WLOS 72
WMBL 123
WNYS 111
WOTB 78
WPTF 122
WRAL 119, 123

WROQ 148	Wild Man 75
WSFL. 123	Williams, Buck. 116
WSKS 107	Williams, Maurice. 3, 154
WSOC. 107, 110	Williams, Woody. 89
WSSB. 120	Wilson, Jackie 21
WTVI 110	Wilson, Rick. 123
"Walk Away Renee" 87	Winburn, Randy 117
Walker, Jr.. 62	Wingate, Mike 21, 91, 101
Walker, Junior 17, 62	Wings 145
Walters, Pat. 16, 19, 20, 25, 46, 47, 48, 49, 51, 52, 57, 58, 59, 60, 68, 84, 86, 87, 106, 109, 110, 115, 129, 140, 141, 145, 146, 155	Winter's Children 76
	"Wipe Out". 22, 39, 71, 82, 108
	Woodstock. 96, 125, 129, 139
Ward, Jim 120	"Wooly Bully" 16
Ward's 44	Words Of Luv. 74
Warner Brothers 43	"World Without Love" 124
Warner-Curb 126	Wray, Link 3
Warwick, Carlton 122	Wunz. 70
Waters, Muddy 1	Wyndam, Freddy. 84, 134
Watson, Dave. 8	
Watson, Merle 116	

Y

"We Ain't Got Nothin' Yet" 87	YMCA. 28, 84
We Gotta Get Out Of This Place" 108	Yager, Denny 38
The Web ..28, 33, 35, 51, 58, 61, 83, 84, 88, 94	Yandle, Marty. 38
Wesley's. 89	Yardbirds 19, 20, 27, 49, 84, 89, 106
West, Tom. 139	Yellow Rose 144
West, Wayne. 110	"You Better Move On" 23
West Charlotte High School 107	Young Ages. 28, 39, 40, 55, 68, 87, 95, 96, 111, 129, 150
West Side Melons 130, 131	
"What I'd Say" 108	Young Ones 122, 123
"Whatzit" 77, 78	Young Rascals 122
"Where Are You". 122	Youngbloods 67
"Where Did I Go Wrong?" 11	

Z

Where The Action Is. 106	Zanadu Coffeehouse. 8
"Whipping Post" 80	Zappa, Frank 67
Whitaker, Chuck. 28, 65, 139	Zero Davis 124
White Whale Records. 124	Zodiacs 3
"A Whiter Shade Of Pale". 82	Zombies 19, 106
Who. 17, 24, 29, 30, 63, 79, 123	

www.ingramcontent.com/pod-product-compliance
Lightning Source LLC
Chambersburg PA
CBHW080544170426
43195CB00016B/2677